MW00411900

Management
OF INTERPRETIVE SITES

Developing Sustainable Operations Through Effective Leadership

Tim Merriman
Lisa Brochu

interpPress

THE
NATIONAL
ASSOCIATION FOR
INTERPRETATION

P.O. Box 2246
Fort Collins, CO 80522

NAI is a private nonprofit [501(c)3] organization and
professional association. NAI's mission is: "Inspiring
leadership and excellence to advance heritage
interpretation as a profession." For information, visit
www.interpnet.com.

ISBN 1–879931–17–6

Contents

Foreword

You wake up one morning to discover you are no longer simply a field interpreter. Your list of job duties now includes budget oversight, fund-raising, supervising staff, creating a strategic plan, performance reviews, maximizing objectives and much more.

You are an interpretive manager. Amid paperwork, forms, and meetings, the trees, birds, or historic artifacts you dedicated your career to interpreting seem very far away.

Most of us who have moved through the ranks of various agencies or organizations into administrative positions do so without ever having any formal training in management techniques. Fortunately, many of these skills, like storytelling or first-person historical character presentations, can be learned. This book provides a knowledge base to assist new and seasoned managers.

It can be daunting to try to live up to excellence in organizational management. But for those who choose this path, the rewards are exciting. Perhaps now your rewards come less frequently from a child holding a butterfly than from the satisfaction of staging an entire special event on butterflies, complete with collaborative partners and sponsors. Professional fulfillment may now come from seeing your staff grow new skills or charting your team's revenue and attendance on an uphill curve.

I am sometimes asked what advice I'd give to interpretive managers. I have three tips for success:

- Do good work and inspire excellence in your staff.

- Keep on top of trends in the fields of interpretation, park management, and even recreation. We can learn much from related disciplines and it makes us better communicators.

- Interpret interpretation.

Think about that last item for a moment. Interpretation strives to connect the audience with the resource. As an interpretive manager you have an obligation to communicate the value of interpretation (a resource in the broader sense) to your audience of park administrators, property managers, and supervisors above you. As Tim Merriman and Lisa Brochu remind us, that's a crucial audience interpreters sometimes miss.

Inside the covers of *Interpretive Management* is an overview of tasks and techniques managers can add to their tool box. There is, however, one tool only you can provide. It might be a magnifying glass or binoculars, a sweep net, tin snips, or any number of gadgets you have used as an interpreter to explore the natural and cultural resources around you.

This book helps you look at the proverbial forest—the big picture. But don't forget to make time to look at the trees—the prairies and the rivers, the stone hearths, and the spinning wheels. Find ways to connect yourself with the resources and rejuvenate your spirit. It will make you a happier, and better, manager.

Evelyn Kirkwood
President
National Association for Interpretation
June, 2004

Preface

Welcome to the challenging world of interpretive management. Management of interpretive sites requires skill in business practices, supervision abilities, and leadership much like any other management challenge. The difference is that managing an interpretive site often means managing the visiting public, interpreters, and some resource significant to our cultural or natural heritage on top of the other more mundane management duties.

Managers of interpretive sites come from varied backgrounds. Interpretive managers are often program specialists, interpreters, guides, naturalists and historians who grew into the management role, although some interpretive managers come from business backgrounds in other fields. Interpretive managers bring passion for their work and skill with it to the tasks of shepherding resources and people into doing a better job. Most managers who grew into the role from a field position realize at some point that much is missing from their formal training and background for being a manager.

No matter what their background, interpretive managers all have the interpretive approach to communication in common. They share a process that is used with diverse resources in extremely varied settings. They share the challenge of thoughtful management. When they manage well, their often limited financial and human resources accomplish more. If they are wasteful, disorganized, and scattered in leadership and management, less gets done. Most managers know of the "Peter Principle" but few admit they might have taken a promotion beyond their abilities. Indeed, being a bit over their heads is a reasonable situation for a new manager. It simply becomes the time to learn again, to apply curiosity and desire to adapt to budgets, planning, personnel management, marketing, evaluation, and sundry other skills.

This book provides insights gathered from our experience in management of government, not-for-profit, and commercial ventures related to interpretation. Between us, we have a little over sixty years of experiences to draw on, but neither of us considers ourselves the ultimate experts. We still learn new things every day, just as every good manager should, from observing other innovators, reading everything we can get our hands on, and partnering with those who complement our own strengths. Staying on the cutting edge means constantly examining and trying new ideas and ways of doing things.

We hope this book will provide a starting place for new managers and a review with perhaps some new approaches for experienced managers. Ultimately, it is the decision-maker at any interpretive site who will make or break the success of that site. It's up to the manager to make the best decisions he or she can in support of his or her agency mission. If we can, in some small way, help managers make better decisions, then perhaps we can be a part of ensuring the health of heritage resources.

You will find the text of the book contains a variety of case studies. These anecdotes are as accurate as we can make them, but reflect our observations alone of any given situation. We know that examples help all of us apply principles and we have tried to share situations that have a lesson of value braided within the story. We hope these help you connect with the real challenges of management while also learning more about theoretical approaches, concepts, and management processes.

The chapter sequence is designed to lead you through management lessons in a very logical way, but you should skip around as you wish. The index, table of contents, and illustrations each have their own values when you are looking for an answer to an immediate question.

We encourage all interpretive managers to stay in touch with their profession. The National Association for Interpretation and many other professional organizations strive to provide new resources, innovative approaches, and provocative ideas in a steady dose. Develop a network of friends and colleagues and keep talking to each other. We really are in this together. Working alone is common in school but rare in the real world. Join us in creating more functional workplaces that can better serve as stewards of our global resource heritage.

If you feel we have missed an opportunity, led you astray on an issue or simply not made our point, feel free to contact us by e-mail with your views. We are always collecting thoughts for revisions in the next edition. Questions are always welcome. You can reach us at:

Tim Merriman, timffortcollins@aol.com
Lisa Brochu, lbrochu@aol.com

Planning

1

If you fail to plan, then plan to fail. Those wise words from an unknown source should be every administrator's credo. Successful businesses, agencies, organizations, and individuals can usually trace their success to a plan that guides their decision-making. A variety of planning strategies can be employed to help solve immediate or long-term challenges. Picking the right strategy for your needs is the first step towards success. Before beginning any planning effort, ask yourself what you're trying to achieve. The answer to that question will reveal what type of planning strategy you need to initiate.

Recognize that plans serve a number of functions. They focus your thinking, identify challenges, suggest solutions for those challenges, provide guidelines for operations, get projects under way, test ideas, and give benchmarks for evaluating success. The type of planning you need to do depends on what problem you're trying to solve. Most plans share some common elements, such as a clear statement of mission, goals, and objectives. But different types of plans focus on different aspects of your operation. In this chapter, a variety of planning strategies with which managers of interpretive sites should be familiar are presented.

Outcomes-Based Management

No matter what type of planning you do, think in terms of outcomes. A plan without clearly written, measurable indicators of success is difficult to implement and impossible to evaluate. But before you can determine what those specific indicators should be, make sure you understand the mission and goals of your organization. Knowing your mission can keep you from spending time and other valuable resources on projects that may be inappropriate for your organization. A mission statement provides a framework for all activities of the organization and should be referred to frequently as a touchstone to ensure that resources are being applied in appropriate ways.

Planning should always support the mission. If you do not know or cannot articulate your organization's mission statement in a simple sentence, your first

Reinforce management messages through a variety of means and in a number of locations for maximum impact.

planning step will be to revisit and clarify that statement. A good mission statement will usually have three components framed in an easily remembered phrase or sentence. Every employee within your organization should be able to repeat the mission statement without referring to a written document or stumbling through the usual litany that begins with, "It's something about...." Put simply, the mission statement should answer the questions: "What is it that we do?", "Whom do we do it for?", and "How do we do it?" Furthermore, it should answer those questions in a dozen words or fewer, if possible.

In identifying the audience, use terms like regional, national, international, or city-wide to define a geographic scope, or families, children, seniors to define a target market. These terms are some examples of general audience descriptions suitable for a mission statement. It is not necessary to get extremely specific with the audience description at this point, but you should have a sense of whom you are serving with your products or services. Identifying the audience keeps you from trying to be or do all things for all people.

Welcome to the

TEXAS STATE AQUARIUM

Our Vision:
To inspire appreciation and wise stewardship of the
Gulf of Mexico

We are:
A private, not-for-profit institution.
We receive no operating funds from the city or state.
Your admission fee helps support our education and
wildlife rehabilitation programs.

Thank you for visiting us.
We appreciate your support

Your mission statement and vision are the very reasons for your existence. Make sure that visitors know what they are by placing them prominently in view and reinforcing the message throughout your operations.

Examples

We bring history alive for eastern Wyoming's children.

Educating people about the world's oceans.

Putting Middleton's residents in touch with nature through research, conservation, and interpretation.

Your primary product or service should also be stated in general terms, but it is perhaps the most important part of the mission statement. The product or service is the heart of your organization. It is why you are in business.

Finally, your mission statement should indicate how you deliver your primary product or service to your audience. General terms that may be appropriate for describing the delivery system might include research, education, interpretation, experiences, training, or sales.

The mission statement gives you an opportunity to sum up the purpose of your organization. It's an important part of any planning process because it provides the parameters within which you can plan. Once you've clearly established your mission, you can begin to articulate goals and measurable objectives that will help you manage your site based on specific outcomes.

Goals should support the mission and be written in general terms. Objectives, on the other hand, should relate to goals and be written in specific, measurable terms. Managers often fall back on measuring only outputs. The number of visitors through the gate, the number of programs delivered, the amount of sales, and the number of brochures distributed are all examples of outputs. While it is certainly important to track outputs, these numbers do not tell you anything about what you've really accomplished. To measure effectiveness, you should attempt to define outcomes, or changes, that occur because of the outputs. For example, if you contact 10,000 visitors this year with flyers about your petroglyph program and 7,500 actually attend (outputs), what happens because of that? Let's say you get 1,000 visitors who attend the program to purchase a petroglyph book in your shop and 500 to sign a pledge that they will help protect the petroglyphs in the park. These are measurable outcomes that illustrate an action or behavior change. Now if you take this concept one step further, you can measure impacts as well. If people understand the significance of the resource and care about it, they are more likely to care for it. So a measurable impact might be the level of reduction of vandalism to the petroglyphs in the park. Thinking in terms of outputs, outcomes, and impacts can help you frame measurable objectives that matter. When budget time rolls around, you are more likely to gain support for your programs if you can demonstrate the impacts that they have. Tom Marcinkowski suggests that logic models with three level of objectives are also being used to analyze environmental education programs.

Regardless of the type of planning you pursue, get in the habit of starting with a clear statement of your mission and goals. As the planning process unfolds, performance objectives appropriate to that process will become evident. Train each of your staff members to develop measurable objectives for every aspect of their jobs and you will soon have a "grade card" that will help you determine effectiveness throughout the site's operations. Planning is all about knowing where you are going, how you intend to get there, and how you did at the end of the journey. Because planning can be one of the most important management tools you can master, it is well worth spending the time and effort to get it right.

Marketing Plan

The marketing plan is used to identify and test new products, programs, or services. It suggests the placement, pricing, publics, and promotion strategies necessary for the product, program or service to be successful. It can also be used for evaluation and revision of existing products, programs, or services. The marketing plan usually includes:

- *Objectives.* Specific, measurable targets for development, implementation, and evaluation of the product, program or service (these objectives should relate directly to a stated goal that reflects the mission of the site)

- *Analysis of Targeted Markets.* An investigation of the market climate and description of the specific niche this product, program, or service will fill

- *Product, Program, or Service Description.* This description should be detailed enough to give readers a clear understanding of what is being proposed or evaluated

- *Pricing Strategy.* Should include a comparison with comparable products to help in determining how much people will pay and explain any pricing assumptions

- *Promotional Opportunities.* Identification of media outlets and other advertising and promotion strategies

- *Budget.* An accounting of expenses required to launch and maintain the program, product, or service and return anticipated on that investment

- *Testing and Revision Strategy.* Evaluation instruments for validating success or understanding failure

A marketing plan should be considered an automatic and necessary part of program or product development to ensure that the new program or product is appropriate for the site and has a real chance of success before investment of staff, financial, or physical resources.

It is also recommended that a marketing and promotions plan be prepared for the site as a whole. This effort can and probably should be done in combination with master planning or interpretive planning, but many sites elect to complete a marketing and promotions plan as a separate piece, especially if a new image or branding strategy needs to be created. In this case, it is often appropriate to work with a marketing or advertising firm, but an interpretive specialist should be included on the planning team to ensure that the firm's approach is consistent with basic interpretive principles and the thematic content of the site.

For additional information on marketing, refer to Chapter 5.

Strategic Plan

A strategic planning process can help you identify strengths, weaknesses, opportunities, and threats to your site's successful operation. The most effective strategic plans will come out of a group process facilitated by an experienced and objective planner. For the best results, facilitation of this process should be handled by someone outside your staff or agency unless there are specific reasons to do otherwise. Strategic planning should not be confused with operations planning. Ideally, strategic planning is a way to define or refine the mission and goals of an organization or to solve a specific problem. Consequently, it should be used when substantial change is needed to guide a group through a process resulting in group commitment to strategies for accomplishing that change. The danger in using a strategic planning process every two to three years as a replacement for operations planning is that changes in leadership, such as those that occur where boards or governance change every year or so, can cause a lack of continuity and commitment to the mission.

Comprehensive Master Plan

When your site was first developed, a comprehensive master plan was probably undertaken that listed significant resources, stated a mission, defined goals and objectives, provided details about architectural, landscape, and interpretive features, and listed necessary operational resources and action items to implement the plan. A good master plan will blend all these elements in a thematic approach that ultimately results in a complete and high-quality visitor experience that can be reasonably supported by management without damage to the resource.

Unfortunately, many sites never revisit their comprehensive master plan once facilities are built and operations are under way. But a master plan does much more than guide initial construction. It should be a living document that reflects the growth and changes that naturally occur over time at any site. Going through a master planning process every five to eight years is an exercise that allows for both continuity and change. The comprehensive master plan is your site's blueprint for success in every area of operations.

Interpretive Plan

The interpretive plan provides guidance for the interpretive program at your site. Generally, if your site includes interpretation, you should have an interpretive master plan that considers all aspects of your program, including personal services and non-personal media. It may be part of the comprehensive master plan or undertaken separately; however, it should always reflect guidance put forth by the comprehensive master plan if such a document exists.

The interpretive master plan should be updated at least every five years, but within that master plan, you might also have specific plans for exhibits, signs, publications, personal services, or other aspects of your program that reflect individual projects to be accomplished or reviewed on an annual or project by project basis.

Since each site's needs are quite different, it is virtually impossible to provide a template for interpretive planning. Although agency templates are a favored way to encourage consistency between sites within a specific agency, such planning methods tend to limit creativity and result in "cookie-cutter" programs that are ineffective because they do not reflect the needs of a site's particular markets or management issues. Nevertheless, certain items can and should be considered in

Thoughtful planning can help you avoid spending money on media that will be underutilized.

every interpretive planning project, whether it is a system-wide planning effort or limited to a single exhibit or trail. These elements, discussed in detail in *Interpretive Planning: The 5-M Model for Successful Planning Projects* by Lisa Brochu, include:

- *management.* mission, goals, objectives, key issues, operational resources (budget, staffing, facilities, equipment, etc.)

- *markets.* analysis of market climate including competitive/complementary sites, assessment of demand, and designation of target markets

- *message.* significant resources, central theme, subthemes, storylines

- *mechanics.* the design balance between facilities, site, and interpretive media and the physical characteristics that might impact development or implementation of interpretation

- *media.* how your message will be communicated to visitors

Business Plan

Anyone who manages interpretive sites can use this approach to attain strategic goals. An annual business plan becomes the road map that leads you to the goals identified in the strategic plan. These two plans, more than any others, work hand in glove to provide guidance for your operations.

A business plan makes it easier to manage the stress of meeting financial and program goals on a daily basis, year in and year out. Because you will know where you are going through the establishment of indicators along the way, you will know what success looks like when you get there.

Private, for-profit businesses have been required for decades by banks and private lenders to deliver business plans to prove that their need and ability to repay are based on sound thinking. The not-for-profit sector readily adapted business planning in recent decades with some modifications. In the past decade, government agencies have also started developing business plans of a more limited scope. Many agencies are restricted from making revenue and some have to turn all revenue over to their governance group. However, with the new mandates for "fee demonstrations" in the federal government and some state governments, park managers and interpretive supervisors face some of the same challenges and opportunities as for-profit and not-for-profit managers. But even if your site must show a zero balance at the end of the year, the business plan can help you figure out how to make that happen.

Elements of a Business Plan

A business plan usually includes the following sections:

- Executive Summary
- Trends Analysis
- Market Environment
- Mission and Goals (aligned with strategic plan)
- Product/Service Analysis
- Budget
- Staffing Plan
- New Initiatives
- Action Plan

It should be simply written and easy to understand so anyone in your organization can use it. Most successful business plans are concise documents of fewer than fifteen pages.

Example:
Table of Contents
   1. Purpose of the Business Plan
   2. Measures of Success
      a. Mission

Market segment	Characteristics	Experience/Service
Primary grade children, Anglo and Hispanic on field trips, low-income families primarily	Kinesthetic learners, short attention span, limited funds for enrichment, some bilingual	Three-hour visit to site: • Puppet show—bilingual • Tour or hike with scavenger hunt • Craft program with take-home souvenir • Anglo and Hispanic on field trips
Seniors—alone or as couples, mostly Anglo, middle and upper-middle income	Love to learn while recreating, great interest in the resource, capable of being donors	Weekday seminars and workshops • Interest-based (i.e. antiques, wildlife, etc.) • Requires limited exertion • Includes opportunity to take ecotour or field trip on longer time basis
Families with young children—middle income suburbanites, all ethnic backgrounds, high-tech professionals	Some with weekday availability and some with weekends only, above average income, want children to learn about history or nature,	Weekday: Parent with child programs of short duration such as storytelling, crafts, and games, etc. Weekend: Parent/child tours or outings of limited time duration—guest artists, musicians, or performers: craft activities, etc.

Sample market segment table for a small museum or nature center

    b. Vision
    c. Core Values
    d. Goals
  3. Existing Conditions
    a. Staffing
    b. Membership
    c. Market Position
    d. Last Year's Action Plan Status
    e. Challenges
  4. New Initiatives
    a. School Programs Expansion
    b. New Facilities/Exhibits
    c. Staff Additions
    d. Partnerships Development
    e. Publication
  5. Budget 20XX
  6. Action Plan 20XX
  7. Addenda
    a. Market Survey
    b. Organizational Chart Last Year
    c. Job Descriptions—new positions
    d. Memorandum of Understanding—partners

Evaluating the Industry or Business/Service Area
A careful study of your industry or business is one of the more difficult parts of the plan because it requires research that may not be easy to obtain, but analyzing trends in the field can provide valuable insights. In the interpretation industry, a variety of trends affect how business is conducted. These trends include:

- Downsizing of government agencies and interpretive staffs
- Privatizing of some services
- Extensive use of volunteer interpreters—docents
- Increased pressure toward revenue development or self-sufficiency
- Increased international tourism globally
- Growth in interest in heritage tourism
- Increased desire of visitors to learn while traveling
- School programming aligned with state standards
- Rapidly increasing transportation costs
- Risk management considerations—potential for terrorism

Trends information is generally available through newspapers, trade papers, professional association articles, research proceedings, and libraries. However, these secondary sources are not nearly so useful as market information derived from specific customer groups. You may wish to conduct the research yourself, if

Interpretation is good management. Interpretive messages on food storage boxes encourage positive behavior change among visitors, ultimately benefiting bears and humans at Yosemite National Park.

you have the ability to do so. If you cannot, encourage nearby universities to study your customers in partnership with you.

At the least, you should be able to make a list of your market segments (customer groups), describe the unique needs and desires of each group, and list or describe how each of your services or products fits these customer groups. A matrix is often a good way to show the relationship between customer groups and the experiences you design to meet their needs.

Making an Honest Evaluation of Your Organization
When you take your own pulse, you have trouble getting an accurate idea of your heart rate. Evaluating your own organization has the same danger. You are too close to the situation and may mistake your own enthusiasm to deliver quality services for customer approval of your services. Feedback from customers can be obtained in myriad ways but it is essential to translate that feedback into information you can use. Evaluation can be approached in a variety of ways:

• External audits—financial analysis of your organization

- Professional audits—visiting experts can give you their views (some options other than hiring consultants include the Institute of Library and Museum Services Museum Assessment Program; Association of Nature Center Administrators Group Consults; and the National Association for Interpretation's Certified Interpretive Planner Course On-site)

- Market research—ongoing surveys of customer views or occasional direct mail samples to compare with earlier surveys

- Focus groups

- Staff logs of questions and inquiries

This portion of the business plan briefly states the strengths and weaknesses of the organization. Infra-structural limitations and needs for equipment, training, and capital projects should be assessed. This section also addresses opportunities in front of the organization based upon the strategic plan. A brief discussion of the mission and long-range goals should be included. A staffing plan should be a part of this section to help you answer the following questions: Do you have the right personnel to meet the challenges of the year? Are there plans to increase or decrease staffing? Will they be assigned differently than before to address this year's action plans?

Fitting the Annual Budget into the Business Plan
The budget or financial plan is one of the most important parts of the business plan. All organizations develop a budget but often no effort is made to demonstrate how it aligns with strategic goals. The description that follows the budget should explain how the budget supports strategic plan goals and meets specific needs in support of the action plan.

The budget should be done as a *pro forma* with monthly expectations for income and expense if there are substantive issues about cash flow. In private, for-profit or not-for-profit organizations, cash flow issues can be very important. It may be necessary to borrow money or transfer funds from other sources during low cash flow periods, but such action should be a planned activity, not a crisis response. Most for-profit and some not-for-profit organizations obtain a line of credit (an open loan account with an upper limit) from their bank for use during low cash flow periods.

Most interpretive organizations have a busy season or seasons. It may not be possible to even out cash flow from month to month, so knowing what funds are available to support activities during the low periods is essential. It is often helpful to put the budget for the next year in the business plan as well. It helps you visualize whether capital reserves will be adequate to increase staff, purchase equipment, and make investments in buildings or infrastructure for a more extended period.

If making income is an essential part of your plan, this section should

Action Tasks	Who	Deadline	Indicator
Develop list of local foundations who assist our kind of organization	Executive Director	End of July this year	List with contact information available by July 31
Write two program grants to local foundations for toddlers program	Program Director	End of September this year	$10,000 award by December (Product Indicator)
Evaluate exhibits and rank as to need for refurbishing	College class	End of June this year	Ranked list completed by June 30
Rebuild three exhibits	Operations Manager	End of March next year	Exhibit hall reopens by April 1 (Product Indicator)

Sample product indicator

point out the most important income goals with specific departmental or staff assignments. Somebody has to be responsible for seeing that each goal is met. If multiple people have the responsibility for any one goal, it becomes easy to pass the blame when it is not met. One person should be the identified lead for each major income goal and be prepared to coordinate the details of achieving it.

In implementing of the business plan, it is essential to display monthly income goals and performance. If departments or individuals fall behind, staff meetings become an opportunity to talk about how all staff can help specific segments of the group achieve a goal that is not being met. Dealing with shortfalls early can cause them to disappear later in the budget cycle. The visual display of income goals and results at all times is intimidating at first but it becomes very reinforcing. You can tell on a monthly basis that you are working together toward common goals and objectives.

Getting Your Business Plan into Action
Action plans can simply be a list of the tasks to be done in the coming year. The action plan should include definite outcomes related to the budget and strategic goals. Each plan item must have a deadline for completion, an assignment to persons who will do the tasks, and process or product outcomes that provide specific measures for achievement.

Process indicators are items that are not final outcomes. If you must send out 10,000 brochures about a program to promote it by a certain date, the date for getting the mailing done is a process indicator. The mailing is not the desired result, but it is an important step to achieve the result. If the program is expected to result in 500 persons signing up, then 500 is one kind of product indicator. The product indicators can be the final registration number and the total income achieved. If the program is expected to make $20,000, that amount is also a product indicator. It is measurable, and you know that it has been achieved or not completely achieved (i.e., "school programs revenue of $20,000 by December 31").

Bookkeeping, record keeping, and program logs must support the action plan. If you are going to monitor progress toward goals on a monthly basis throughout the year, the records have to be updated monthly and reported to staff in a meeting where shortfalls and accomplishments can be discussed and celebrated, respectively. And it is important to celebrate making your goals— hitting the product indicators. Parties, awards, gifts, and verbal expressions of thanks can all be a part of the reinforcement that keeps everyone interested in making the outcomes a reality. For-profit organizations often pay bonuses for goals achieved and many not-for-profits and even some government agencies have also adopted this practice. If the regulations of an organization do not prohibit the use of a financial incentive, it can be an effective motivator for achievement of goals.

Making one person the champion of each action plan item allows a clear means of working on completion of tasks, as each person on the team knows his or her specific assignment in the plan.

Implementation Guidelines
Some general guidelines for successful implementation follow:

- The plan reads well and each section builds on the logic of the preceding one.

- The plan does not contain unneeded detail or fluff.

- Staff are involved in writing it and believe the goals can be achieved.

- Copies are provided to everyone on staff and among governance who might need it.

- It is more functional than pretty.

- Goals are "outcomes" or "results" oriented.

- Goals are a "stretch" but not "miracle territory."

- Everyone involved knows his/her specific assignments.

- The plan is an active document referred to throughout the year.

- A monthly report keeps staff and governance updated on progress.

Monthly reporting on progress of the action plan is one of the easiest ways to keep the details of the plan in mind. If you want your governance group (board, boss, or investors) to monitor that progress, you should copy them on the report. An easier way to report to a group that includes board, staff and partners is to create a report that is posted on the Internet monthly. This electronic grade card gives each interested person a place to look at the same time monthly. It is reassuring to see progress and instructive to study the areas in which you need to improve to achieve goals.

Helpful Resources

Brochu, Lisa. *Interpretive Planning: The 5-M Model for Successful Planning Projects.* InterpPress: Fort Collins, CO. 2003.

Covello, Joseph, and Brian Hazelgren. *Your First Business Plan: 2nd Edition.* Sourcebooks, Inc.: Naperville, IL. 1995.

Mancuso, Joseph R. *How to Prepare and Present a Business Plan.* Fireside-Simon & Schuster: New York, NY. 1992.

Marcinkowski, Thomas. *Monograph 1—Using a Logic Model to Review and Analyze an Environmental Education Program.* North American Association for Environmental Education: Washington D.C. 2004.

Patterson, Carol. *The Business of Ecotourism.* Explorer's Guide Publishing: Rhinelander, WI. 1997.

Tiffany, Paul, and Steven D. Peterson. *Business Plan for Dummies.* IDG Books Worldwide, Inc.: Foster City, CA. 1997.

Personnel Management

It has been said that great managers do things right and great leaders do the right things. As an interpretive manager, you have an opportunity to be both a great manager and a great leader. Doing things right will demand that you continue to build your personal tool kit of skills—budget management, business planning, marketing, personnel management, and more, but leadership requires more than competencies.

Leadership in Natural and Cultural Resource Settings

Dr. Corky McReynolds at University of Wisconsin–Stevens Point studied successful nature center directors in the early 1990s and compiled their comments based on commonalities. He found three very compelling leadership traits among those who had proven themselves in the field. Leaders have a passion for people, they have a passion for purpose, and they are vision-driven.

The first trait may seem obvious. Leadership involves working with people. If you truly enjoy working with others, challenging them to do their best, and you have a passion for people, you can accomplish wonders. It is a key ingredient. It's hard to fake it if you're not a "people" person.

Passion for purpose is less obvious. Many interpretive organizations don't have a stated mission. Yet leaders at the studied nature centers were passionate about their organization's purpose even if it was not stated in print. They had a sense of what their organization was about and pursued it with enthusiasm. The value of a written mission statement is that it ensures everyone's passion is pointed the same direction.

If you do not know where you are going, every road will get you nowhere.

—Henry Kissinger

Vision-driven was the third very important trait of these leaders. They each had a vision of the long-term destination of her or his organization, five or ten years out. They knew where the organization should be headed and worked to inspire others to share that vision.

Austrian psychologist Viktor Frankl survived the Nazi death camps and wrote about the meaning of life in later years. He observed, "When we are no longer able to change a situation, we are challenged to change ourselves." Many other traits are important but vision and a sense of a personal mission—a need to accomplish things in the future—were the most vital and important.

Leadership is the capacity to translate vision into reality.

—Warren G. Bennis

How do we translate that vision into reality? We work shoulder to shoulder with people, inspiring them one at a time.

I start with the premise that the function of leadership is to produce more leaders, not more followers.

—Ralph Nader

Sometimes you lead best when you follow Tom Sawyer's example and get others to paint the fence or even organize friends to paint the fence. Not-for-profit and governmental interpretive organizations are built on the stewardship of volunteers and docents. An estimated 500,000 volunteers, docents, seasonals, and front-liners work as interpreters in the United States, perhaps twice that many in the world. Your role as a leader is to help them see the vision and inspire them to pursue it with you, using all of your minds and hands collectively.

It can be frustrating with too few resources and too much to do. But anything is possible.

Never doubt that a small group of thoughtful, concerned citizens can change the world. Indeed it is the only thing that ever has.

—Margaret Mead, twentieth-century anthropologist

A passion for people and purpose helps engage others to pursue a vision, a destination only imagined. And when that vision becomes reality, another vision of the future appears, but unlike a mirage in the desert, it does not disappear as it is embraced. It simply spawns another vision. With humility and caring you, as a leader, engage others to pursue and participate in your visions. And if you listen to others, their ideas become part of the visioning process. Strategic planning provides a structure for bringing your ideas and those of others together into a common vision.

Make no little plans! They have no magic to stir men's blood.

—Daniel Burnham, nineteenth-century Chicago architect

A good manager leads by example, whether training staff, handling daily business functions, or dealing directly with visitors. (Pictured: Evie Kirkwood)

Media giant Robert Edward "Ted" Turner III said that his father urged him to always have a dream, one that's a stretch. He once dreamed he would manage the world's most powerful media organization. He admitted that he was the most surprised when he attained that vision before turning fifty. After achieving that he set out to "save the Earth." He now owns almost two million acres of land, has 32,000 head of bison and is devoted to exemplary land management. His son Beau is following in his conservation-minded footsteps.

You can amaze yourself when you reach beyond your grasp and then find your vision within your outstretched palm. Your leadership multiplies your limited energy a thousand-fold and passion fires the process.

Passion, though a bad regulator, is a powerful spring.
> —Ralph Waldo Emerson, nineteenth-century American essayist,
> public philosopher, and poet

As a manager, you may often find yourself caught in the web of the urgent but unimportant details of daily tasks. They seem to eat you alive, commanding your attention. Your dreams are obscured by the daily melee. But you have an opportunity every single day to reinvent yourself. Bishop Tutu points out that some people become leaders through circumstance. For others, leadership comes with age, knowledge and empowerment. This awareness of what it takes to lead will give you tools and the permission to improve your leadership skills. Sometimes leadership is as simple as letting your passion show and your ideas be known. Getting involved in your professional association, church, or local youth organization as a volunteer leader supports what you do at your work. You can exercise your leadership abilities in a variety of places. You may still have to take care of the details, but it will not be all that you do.

The passion of shared vision empowers people to transcend the petty, negative interactions that consume so much time and effort and deplete quality of life.
—Stephen R. Covey, author

Character and Competencies
Character is like a tree and reputation like its shadow. The shadow is what we think of it; the tree is the real thing.
—Abraham Lincoln, nineteenth-century U.S. president

The character of an interpretive manager is vitally important as with all professionals. Your efforts to be honest, responsible, ethical, and fair are being observed by your staff and you greatly influence your organizational culture. You cannot expect them to be honest while you treat the truth flexibly to achieve your ends in dealing with others.

If you study the business community, you know that many civic organizations have found ways to remind their members of a commitment to ethical practices. Rotary International uses "The 4-Way Test of the Things We Say and Do":

Is it the truth?

Is it fair to all concerned?

Will it build goodwill and better friendships?

Will it be beneficial to all concerned?"

They remind members of the test at meetings and give guests and friends gifts with the "4-Way Test" embossed on them. They also have a program where the test is shared with high school students as part of Rotary's commitment to the community and to ethical practices in business. They are aware that a culture of character does not just happen. It's important to talk about character issues with staff and colleagues. Your management interests must be more than budgets, business plans, products, and services.

Unless someone like you cares a whole awful lot, nothing is going to get better. It's not.
—Dr. Seuss, *The Lorax*

One way you can keep from becoming lost among management details without seeing the overall impact of what you do is to get involved in a local civic organization like Rotary, Kiwanis, Lions Club, or Optimists. They all consider community networking, service work, and continuing education to be important parts of character development. It also allows you to share the good work of your organization with the community on a regular basis. It takes time and some money but the investment of both are worthwhile.

Your tenure as a leader is dependent upon your personal ethical foundation. Those who have given you responsibilities expect a fundamental honesty and allegiance to the mission of your agency, organization, or business. Each stakeholder expects fair and consistent treatment. On a daily basis your personal values are judged by your staff, partners, supervisors, colleagues, and customers. You lead best by example. You often hear, "You must walk the talk," in reference to the importance of displaying your beliefs in your own ethical principles by showing them in action. Your credibility slides away when you give lip service to ethical values and demonstrate something different.

Your honesty as an ethical professional is not guaranteed by having a written code of ethics, but that is sometimes a good idea. It's a reminder to others and to yourself that you have well-defined beliefs that you are willing to demonstrate to the community in speech and action, like the Rotary 4-Way Test. Displaying the code of ethics in the office or asking staff members to sign a copy of it declares for all how important it is to you as the manager.

The function of education is to teach one to think intensively and to think critically.... Intelligence plus character—that is the goal of true education.
—Martin Luther King Jr., Nobel Prize-winning twentieth-century American civil rights leader

The mark of a true professional in any field is the personal commitment to self-improvement. There is always more to know and there is always value to learning from others. That cannot be just a commitment to your own growth. All staff deserve the opportunity to develop to their full potential. Make a personal growth plan for professional development a basic part of your organizational culture. Developing human resources to their fullest potential is vital to your success as a leader and to your agency or organization.

Personal Growth

Professional associations like the National Association for Interpretation (NAI) are another place to continue your education. Market research in NAI has indicated that members join to network with colleagues and gain new

New and experienced interpreters benefit from NAI's Certified Heritage Interpreter courses. Many organizations now require interpreters to be certified by NAI.

skills and competencies. To be a good leader and manager you need as many tools in your personal tool kit as possible. Mastery of new software, knowledge of planning approaches, and the study of evaluative methods are just a few examples of the many skills you can pursue best by learning from colleagues. You can continually reinvent the wheel or visit a wheelwright and learn how much is already known.

Certification credentials are the newest educational and evaluation programs in the interpretive profession. NAI offers credentials such as Certified Interpretive Host, Certified Interpretive Guide, Certified Heritage Interpreter, Certified Interpretive Manager, Certified Interpretive Trainer, and Certified Interpretive Planner. Earning a certification credential, like earning a degree, is not an end but simply another beginning. You prove yourself against the standards of the profession with evaluation by your peers. To re-certify you must show that you have continued to take seminars and attend professional workshops. NAI's certification program and similar opportunities are described in greater detail in Chapter 9.

Freeman Tilden said that he viewed education as a lifelong process. As a leader and manager, you should consider yourself to be on a journey of continual self-discovery and self-improvement. You reveal the richness of your own character when you show in small, everyday ways your commitment to fairness and honesty while trying to improve yourself. Personal growth can be through a civic club, a professional association or a distance-learning course.

One of the side benefits is more emotional than intellectual. The petty quarrels, bureaucratic frustrations, and conflicts in everyday life can slowly erode your resolve to do your work. Professional burnout is a very real problem. Your professional network is a potential solution and workshops are places to rekindle your inner fire. Friends made at meetings and training are there for you when you need them.

Professional Development, Recognition, and Rewards

As a manager, you have an opportunity to be a catalyst for professional development among your employees. You can help them realize their fullest potential in a variety of ways. Your organization benefits when they grow in skills and abilities. Several ways to encourage professional development are:

- Ask each employee to identify their professional objectives for the year in the performance review document you use and discuss progress toward it quarterly.

- Allocate funds in the budget for attending workshops or seminars and let each one know how much is available for her or his professional development.

- Allocate matching funds for them to join professional organizations so that they have an investment in it and know that you value their participation.

- Encourage attainment of certification by giving a bump in pay or a few days off when a credential is earned.

- Recognize employee achievements in your organizational newsletter or on a bulletin board so that they know you value their accomplishments.

- Ask your boss or governance body for approval to give cash bonuses to staff for meeting and surpassing annual objectives in the business plan.

- Present awards or bonuses in front of other employees to let all know how important you believe professional achievement is.

- Celebrate employee birthdays, milestones with the organization (five years, ten years, etc.), and earned credentials with parties, special lunches, or special gifts to let all know that there are times to relax and play.

Some organizations permit only one staff member to attend a professional meeting or workshop. They ask that person to relate to other staff what they learned upon return. That approach may make sense financially, but it ignores the emotional component of being a professional. If workshops and meetings were only about content, it could all be done through distance learning. People are social beings and sharing with colleagues and the revitalization that results from it will not be accomplished at a distance or in a secondhand way. Managers who do not nurture the professional growth of their employees are not getting the most out of their human resources. You maintain your vehicle if you want it to work well when you need it. The maintenance of people requires a similar investment in their psychological and intellectual well-being.

Recognition and awards also matter very much. Recognition may not be a primary motivation but it makes a difference to know that others recognize efforts. Visible awards turn praise into something tangible and lasting. Employees can share these icons of success with their families, peers, and friends. Awards provide reinforcement for behaviors you want to nurture. They reassure employees that they are doing what is expected and more. People are both intellectual and emotional beings and recognition addresses our emotional needs with a lasting pat on the back.

Internal Audiences

Many marketing specialists will tell you that you must be sensitive to the needs of your audience. But the external markets, those people who use your services, are only one segment you need to consider. Internal markets, or audiences, are those who support your efforts as a manager. The boss or governance group is one obvious internal audience. The business plan and monthly or quarterly reports are designed to keep her or him or them in the loop. They need to be constantly reminded that you know the objectives of the organization and work toward achieving them.

Supervisors also need rewards and recognition. If someone in supervision of your program does something particularly supportive, think about recognizing him or her at an agency or organizational meeting. It may be the difference in that support being there or not being there the next time you need it. The National Association for Interpretation has an award for supportive administrators that can be nominated by their subordinates. You can make that nomination and get recognition for your managers from a national organization, which also makes your boss more aware that you are not just involved locally, but with colleagues from the entire nation.

Employees and volunteers are another important internal audience, as are contractors, temporary employees, and seasonal workers. Some believe they are the most important audience in some ways.

How many of you ever heard a boss or supervisor say, "The customer comes first." A recent book, *The Customer Comes Second and Other Secrets of Exceptional Service* by Hal F. Rosenbluth and Diane McFerrin Peters, suggests that employees come first. It's challenging to get employees to treat visitors or customers in a manner unfamiliar to them. Honesty, open communication, and consistency are values you might want shared with visitors. That's more likely to happen if you treat employees honestly, openly, and consistently.

Employees who hear you lie, see you cover up a mistake, or shunt responsibility for an error onto someone who is not present will feel similarly comfortable in doing that with their publics. As a manager, you create a culture—a culture of honesty or deceit, open or shrouded, consistent or erratic. You choose on a daily basis to shape and reinforce that culture.

No one knows you as well as your employees, especially those who report to you. Making them feel valued and trusted is essential. They represent you in your absence. They pass on the values you share with them to their employees, volunteers, and customers. Your example in how you manage is more powerful than anything you say. Your body language screams your real beliefs.

Coaching

If you deliberately plan on being less than you are capable of being, then I warn you that you'll be unhappy for the rest of your life.

—Abraham Maslow

Think back to your childhood. Who made a difference in your life? Who helped you become who you are? Everyone has mentors or coaches in their past—people who were the catalysts in helping them become the best that they could be. How did they do that? Did they scream and yell at you? Did they make demands without giving you explanations? Most people simply do not respond well to the old-fashioned dictatorial teacher, boss, or parent. They want those who supervise them to respect their intelligence and help them understand the "why" behind what they are asked to do.

You can think of supervision as a continuum ranging from a dictator at one end who makes demands to a coach at the other extreme who makes suggestions. As a manager you choose where you want to fall along that continuum, but you must consider the consequences of that choice.

A good coach will make his players see what they can be rather than what they are.

—Ara Parasheghian

Conflict Resolution

One might as well try to ride two horses moving in different directions, as to try to maintain in equal force two opposing or contradictory sets of desires.

—Robert Collier

A workplace is much like a family gathering. No matter how well everyone seems to like and respect each other on the surface, there will be times when conflict arises. The nature of the conflict dictates what action to take, but the good

Docents (volunteers who act as interpreters) can become a valued part of your workforce, but should be managed by paid staff and trained when they begin working.

manager is prepared to help employees resolve their differences in productive ways. An open policy that encourages employees to talk about issues in a safe environment such as a staff meeting or retreat may provide enough of an opportunity to vent about what may seem to be petty personality conflicts that those minor conflicts can be defused before they become destructive. Many times a disgruntled employee is simply looking for someone to listen to them gripe a bit. But sometimes a more serious problem arises and a more concentrated effort is required. Establish a grievance policy and let everyone know the appropriate ways to handle inter-office conflict.

As a manager, it may be necessary to play the role of peacemaker by bringing both parties into your office for some direct counseling. Allowing both parties to work together under your supervision to determine strategies for resolution may keep the issue from consuming the office or causing other workers to take sides in something that may not even concern them. If you are uncomfortable or unskilled at personnel counseling, investigate the feasibility of bringing in an outside moderator or counselor if the situation warrants that sort of attention.

If one employee seems to be a perpetual problem, constantly complaining, undercutting management's direction, or infecting the workplace with a negative attitude, it may be necessary to follow the appropriate steps in your agency to document the problem and let the person find another place to work where he or she will be happier. Many times, conflict in the workplace can be traced to a single unhappy individual insistent on making everyone else miserable. If that seems to be the case after a careful analysis of the conflicts that come up, then taking action for dismissal may well be the best course of action.

Staffing Plan/Organizational Charts

An organizational chart gives you and others a visual understanding of how you are organized. It also gives you a chance to see your staff in a different way. You should be thinking at least three years into the future about your staffing needs. If the money was available tomorrow, who would you hire and why would you hire them? Would you use a contractor or put on a staff member? Using a contractor offers the advantage of allowing you to test the need for the position for a year or two while developing a plan to support the new staff member. Long-term outsourcing should not include your core businesses—those mission-related activities you do better than others.

The chart also allows you to assess weak areas or overloaded areas if faced with cutbacks. It is a painful thought, but what position would you eliminate if faced with a sudden cutback? With the exception of establishing a general long-range plan for staffing, it may be best not to share your immediate plans for hiring or firing with other staff. A projection of the position to be hired next will sound like a promise to the staff members supported by the new hire. If you talk about getting them help and do not get it done, you have created a problem where none existed.

Contractors and volunteers should also be shown on the staffing plan and organizational chart. They carry a portion of the workload—sometimes a major amount of it. Volunteers can become integral to the operation of interpretive programming, requiring the addition of staff to handle the responsibilities for supervising, scheduling, and training the volunteer group. If volunteers are the front line of the organization, meeting and greeting the public, they must know the mission, goals, and objectives to some degree and understand what you want done.

The National Association for Interpretation created the Certified Interpretive Guide (CIG) and Certified Interpretive Host (CIH) programs for this express purpose. The thirty-two-hour CIG and sixteen-hour CIH training courses bring any new hire or volunteer to a level of competence that supports the organization well. The folks at Disney give new hires one to three weeks of training before putting them in front of their audiences. They know that one rude or ill-prepared employee can ruin the "Disney" magic. Yet other interpretive sites often turn cadres of volunteers loose in parks, zoos, museums, nature centers, and historic sites with minimal training or only content training. It's not enough to know the resource. They must understand the interpretive communication process and how it protects and preserves the resource. They help accomplish your mission when trained properly and may derail it if not trained at all.

Case Study

As a consultant, I am often asked to help plan projects that represent a significant portion of a capital budget. I try to enter into any consulting situation with an open mind and am usually unaware of the office politics that may influence the project. In the interest of efficiency, I've learned to be a good observer of human nature and can usually assess a simmering situation fairly quickly. But I've never believed it's a good idea to hire a consultant without letting him or her know that part of the job may need to be mediation. If you know that ahead of time, let the consultant know what they're in for—using a third party as an objective pair of eyes can be a valuable tool, but when the consultant becomes a pawn in a game of interoffice politics, everybody loses.

In one instance, a nature center hired an exhibit firm to complete a major exhibit design project. I was hired as a "liaison" to the exhibit firm. After an assistant supervisor had refused several rounds of exhibit designs, I questioned him to find out what was wrong. He admitted he was deliberately trying to aggravate his supervisor. In the meantime, he had wasted over $150,000 of the city's money and countless hours of staff time. In another case, I had been hired to develop a marketing plan for a federal site. Before I arrived, the superintendent explained that there appeared to be a "personality conflict" between himself and one of the key decision-makers whose job it would be to carry out the plan. Part of my role as consultant was to counsel the pair through some difficult discussions so that they could come to agreement on key issues. Knowing that as I went into the project enabled me to use their dollars efficiently and arrive at a plan that worked for everybody. The bonus was that communication between them improved dramatically as a result of successful completion of the project, so the entire workplace benefited long after the project was done.

—Lisa Brochu

It is your responsibility to train new hires and the CIG and CIH courses are some of the many ways to accomplish that. The CIG curriculum is designed for those who give interpretive presentations or lead tours, while the CIH curriculum is designed for those who have public contact but who do not give presentations or lead tours (ticket takers, receptionists, maintenance workers, law enforcement, security, sales clerks, etc.).

Managers or program supervisors can seek training through NAI to become a Certified Interpretive Trainer (CIT) with NAI's sanction to teach the CIG and CIH courses. This approach makes using the CIG and CIH curricula more affordable for any organization and gives some assurance that the trainer understands the needs of the organization.

Human resources are vital to your success. You must care for your people if you want them to care for your audiences and the resources. They must feel valued and know that you listen to them. Leadership and management are not about power, but about collaboration. You must plan strategically, hire good people you can trust, and manage by example. When you and your team pull the same direction, you can move or change anything.

Suggested Resources

Rosenbluth, Hal F., Diane McFerrin Peters. *The Customer Comes Second and Other Secrets of Exceptional Service.* Quill/Harper-Collins: New York. 1994.

NAI Certification Study Guide at http://www.interpnet.com.

Time Management

3

You walk up to the car rental counter at a major airport to pick up the vehicle you have reserved weeks in advance. The clerk smiles and says, "Welcome to Rent-a-car," and your process is moving. You'll soon be on the road and rolling. The phone rings, the clerk picks it up and you stand and wait while Rent-a-car's newest customer gets help over the phone and you cool your heels. The urgency of the call trumped the importance of face-to-face customer service. It happens every day in almost every business.

You return from your annual vacation to a huge pile of mail. You sort through it and find a huge marketing survey in the pile. You don't enjoy surveys but you do like the summaries of information that come from them so you ease back into work by completing it while the other mail is left in stacks. Later that day you find out about a grant application deadline this same day, but too little time is left to pursue it. Worse yet it is from a friendly foundation who assures you that your organization will get help if you can just return the paperwork by the deadline. Ouch.

Ben Franklin said, "Never confuse motion with action." Spinning our mental or physical wheels can waste time. Time management is not a new challenge, but there are some new solutions. They all begin with personal change.

Management guru Stephen Covey teaches the "Time Management Matrix" in *The 7 Habits of Highly Effective People*. The book is a good read if you are highly motivated about diving into self-improvement books. If you do not do that well, buy the audio-cassette tapes of the same name and listen to it while driving somewhere. That works better if you are an auditory learner and it passes the time while driving. The matrix Covey shows has "urgent" on the horizontal axis compared to "important" on the vertical axis. He points out that an important item is "contributes to your mission, your values, your high priority goals." Urgent matters "insist on action."

Quadrant 1 includes the most urgent and important activities that serve your mission and also demand your immediate attention. You have an accident victim on your trails. Your board or supervisor just called and must have a report today to get your budget renewed with an appropriate increase. The prescribed burn on your prairie has jumped a firebreak and is burning toward the county's forest preserve and a housing development. Most managers move to these tasks, often dubbed issues, crises, or problems, easily and intuitively. Some such problems are unavoidable and will not disappear no matter what you do. They demand your attention. However if you spend more time in Quadrant 2 working with the non-urgent but important strategies you can reduce the amount of time you spend in crisis management, which is often more expensive because it does not allow thoughtful planning.

Quadrant 2 is where you set your vision, study your audiences, and plan strategies and action plans that will achieve the visions. This is where you can be proactive and search for efficient, effective ways to work. Quadrant 1 is more reactive. You have a problem and must deal with it. But, if you work in Quadrant 2 in a steady manner, you reduce the chances of having the problem over and over again. Quadrant 2 is where you take charge of your life and organization and learn to manage by outcomes. You can use strategic and business planning to map the future instead of being a marionette with varied crises as the puppeteers.

One component of Covey's Quadrant 2 that might surprise you is "recreation." Your mental and physical health is essential to doing a good job. If you are eating a junk food lunch at your desk, skipping the daily jog or walk due to lack of time, and reading e-mails into the dark of night instead of spending time with your family, you may have a heart attack. You must plan to maintain your own mental and physical health. Prevention of health problems is a good investment. Daily recreation prepares you emotionally and physically to be at your best.

Quadrants 3 and 4 may be urgent or non-urgent, but consider the larger picture. They are unimportant. They are tasks that do not advance your mission. If you spend your time sorting junk mail, doing busywork, and returning phone calls to unwanted solicitors, you are not spending that time on activities that will allow you to manage well with an eye on the vision you identified for your future.

Innovation is not just doing new things that matter. It can also mean quitting the things that do not help you get where you are going. Leave the quadrant 3 and 4 tasks on the table and not on your daily task list. Spend time in Quadrant 2 planning for the future and developing relationships and opportunities that matter.

Scheduling Systems—Becoming More Efficient and Effective

Every day is a new opportunity to be more efficient and more effective. It often is best to make the first appointment or meeting of the morning thirty minutes or an hour after arrival, not at your arrival time. Take a look at your day's schedule. Study your plans for the day and make a list of what you want to accomplish and prioritize the items on the list. Attempt to allocate time to each task in a realistic manner.

Covey emphasizes that we should be efficient with things but effective with people. He said, "People are more important than things." You may allocate thirty minutes to a meeting with an employee who has a problem and then find that a two-hour discussion ensues that does not get either of you where you need to be in resolving the problem. It's critical that you work with the people in your lives in a thoughtful, caring manner. They are not "things" on your schedule. They are your teammates, your colleagues, and your time with them must be more flexible to support your relationship with them effectively. The outcome must be what you both judge to be just and responsible, not just what you have scheduled.

Being efficient with things may require you to change some habits. You may need a tool that works for you to implement it. Time management tools are varied and those that work for one person may not work for another. One of the most simple ways to keep a task list for the day in mind is to put it on a flip chart in your office, printed large and with checklist boxes to permit you to reinforce yourself by checking them off. The same approach on a computer screen or even sticky notes on your desk can work. The idea is to keep your daily goals in front of you so that you don't become sidetracked.

If you prefer something more official, there are many planner systems available at almost every office supply store. DayTimers™ or Franklin planners are some of the best known, having been adopted by legions of corporate and government road warriors and executives. They have the rich, professional trappings of leather cases and zipper folders with thoughtful printed calendars that are easy on the eyes. And the company will teach you how to use them at seminars, over the Internet, or simply through instructions that come with them. They are neat systems, but not for everyone. You need to use what seems natural and easy for you, not something that seems to be the "in" thing.

The same might be said for Palm Pilots and a wide variety of other personal organizer hardware and software. They are great tools if they work for you. You still have to have your own ideas about how to prioritize to be more efficient and more effective. They can help keep the list, remind you of deadlines, organize data and catalog your ideas. Systems created within software, notebooks, and personal organizers are only good if you use them.

Have More Effective Meetings

That title doesn't mean you should plan additional meetings, just that the ones you must have should be more effective. It's no surprise that one of the most ineffective uses of time is in meetings. Just mention a meeting to your staff and most will roll their eyes and sigh deeply. The key to making a meeting something to look forward to instead of tantamount to torture is in facilitation. Leaderless meetings, like leaderless organizations, are doomed from the start. Learning some simple facilitation tips that will help you take charge of your meetings can turn them into productive time that gets you closer to your achieving your goals, whether they are ten-minute follow-ups or day-long workshops.

Before you schedule a meeting, determine why you're having it and who needs to participate. Many meetings are unnecessary or unproductive because the wrong people attend. It sounds like common sense, but you've probably attended a few of those meetings in your career and wondered why you couldn't have spent that time actually doing something instead. Once you decide a meeting is necessary and you're confident you know who will be there and why, prepare an agenda.

Depending on the meeting, the agenda probably doesn't need to be scheduled to the minute, but you should have a general idea of how much time is available for each of the elements included on the agenda to keep you on track. Post the agenda or pass it out so that everyone in the room knows what you want to accomplish in the amount of time you have. Ask if there are any items the group feels is missing from the agenda and make any revisions necessary to accommodate omissions, if possible, but try not to mix meeting purposes. If there appear to be a number of omissions, maybe another meeting is in order so that you can stay focused on your original agenda.

State the outcomes you expect. Again, ask the group if there are any outcomes that they hope to achieve that have not been stated. Once you have support of the agenda and outcomes, go over any rules for the meeting. Rules will vary according to the meeting, but make it clear how you will solicit input from participants and what sorts of behavior and comments are appropriate. Assign someone to be a timekeeper or keep track of time yourself with an easily visible watch or clock.

If you're having a short session of less than an hour, provide water and make sure everyone's comfortable. If you're having a longer session, offer light refreshments, let everyone know they can get up and stretch if needed, and set the stage for your meeting so that all necessary materials (easel pads, markers, etc.) are at hand. It sometimes helps to provide stress relief toys (squishy balls, koosh balls, etc.) to keep everyone thinking creatively.

Once you get started, keep the meeting moving according to the agenda. Learn to recognize the various roles that emerge in any group dynamic. Some people tend to be "helpers" while others seem intent on hindering the process. Allow the helpers to help, but only under your direction or they may "help" you right out of your agenda and into another issue. Helpers generally seek stability within the group, clarifying thoughts of others or asking for group consensus. They often will neutralize a negative influence in the group by putting a positive spin on a naysayer's comments. As the facilitator, you can channel their positive energy and use it to help move the meeting along.

Handling the more difficult people in the group can be a bit trickier, but is essential to a productive outcome. Making direct eye contact with someone who is intent on disruption is often enough to quell the undesirable behavior, but often someone in the group is verbally combative. Practice gentle ways of allowing such a person to have their say, but pulling the pith out of their comments. Often someone in this mode just needs to say their piece and having said it, will settle down and let you get on with the meeting; however, letting such a person have the floor can take your meeting down a road from which there is no return if you are not watchful. Taking a break is a good way to head them off at the pass. During the break, talk to the individual and see if you can come to agreement about appropriate behavior in the meeting and if not, you may need to suggest that you have a private session with them later so that everyone else can have a productive session.

Be aware that some people who are quiet during meetings are not necessarily disagreeing or disapproving of the proceedings. They may simply feel that they want to listen rather than contribute. Encourage them, but don't force participation. Do make it clear that a group process is only as effective as the group's willingness to participate to fend off later accusations of being ignored or overlooked.

Start and end your meetings on time. Few people will complain if a meeting ends early, but starting late gives the impression that the participants' time is not valuable and may disrupt your agenda right from the start. Allow frequent breaks or give the opportunity for participants to stand up and stretch periodically.

Practice with using visual aids before your meeting. If using slides, use reverse out type on a dark background for best results. If using overheads, use dark type on a light or blank background. For easel pads, use a variety of colored markers to make your points. Use unscented markers to avoid toxic fumes from markers and check to see if your markers will bleed through paper before writing directly on paper attached to a wall. Alternate dark colors such as brown and purple to make it easier for people to see each line distinctly. Use both upper and lower case letters as appropriate, rather than all caps or all lower case. Resist the urge to write in cursive. Printed letters are much easier to read. If you have difficulty spelling, have illegible handwriting, or simply want to remain focused on the group, ask someone in the group to be a recorder. Try to make each letter at least one to two inches tall for the best readability. If you have trouble remembering to write large enough, use the easel pads that are marked with grid lines. The easiest easel pads are the 3-M Post-It™ pads. Although slightly more expensive than regular pads, these pads allow you to post each page on the wall so that they can be seen and referred to throughout the meeting.

No matter what type of meeting you must conduct, be prepared. Your meeting participants will appreciate the sense that you value their time and input and you will begin to see results instead of the analysis paralysis that so often accompanies an unstructured approach to meetings.

Meetings Serve Varied Purposes

Information Meeting or Seminar
The "brown bag lunch" is one example of a very effective and efficient way to hold a regular seminar in your organization. This simple tool is a great way to have ongoing professional development in an organization with a minor commitment

of time and resources. Invite a guest, partner, vendor, contractor, or expert to join you for lunch and talk informally about their expertise or interests. Invite staff and everyone to bring a lunch—thus the name "brown bag"—or have everyone pitch in a few dollars and let a different person head to the deli for a surprise menu each week. It costs little to do this and it builds relationships. This approach requires little facilitation other than someone to introduce the guest who will speak and order a lunch for her or him.

Creative Problem-Solving or Planning Meetings

These meetings are often used for coming up with ideas rather than decisions. Many meetings of this nature will benefit from a brainstorming phase followed by a clarification phase. During the brainstorming session, protect the ideas that are expressed and offer no judgments or you may inadvertently shut down further participation. There will be enough time for weeding out less useful ideas in the clarification phase. Setting priorities or selecting ideas for further consideration can be accomplished through multi-voting techniques, such as 10/4. With this approach, give each participant ten small sticky dots and allow them to vote on their preferences by affixing up to four dots next to their favorite ideas. They can place their dots on any idea they choose, but the total votes per person must not exceed ten, and the total votes allowed for any one idea from any one individual must not exceed four. This approach consistently gets to the heart of the matter through a group consensus process and inappropriate ideas will simply sift to the bottom of the pile.

If issues get brought up that aren't appropriate for the meeting or that you think will take more time to resolve than you have available, write them on a "parking lot" list so the thoughts don't get lost, but make it clear that those issues will have to dealt with at a later time. Allow free expression but gently rein in the group and refocus on the issue at hand when the thought process begins to wander too far afield. If open participation gets out of hand, or you have people who seem reluctant to participate in an open forum, try using a round robin approach, where each person gets to contribute. Successive participants can simply agree if they feel the same way or pass if they haven't yet formed their thoughts. Allow those who pass to speak up after everyone else has completed the round.

Update Meeting

The weekly, monthly, or quarterly staff meeting is one of the more common examples of a management meeting. This meeting is a chance to update staff on progress toward action plan objectives. It's also a good time to congratulate those surpassing objectives and give awards. Staff should have input into the agenda to allow them to talk about their programs and concerns. The Action Agenda outlined below should be used if this is a decision-making meeting, but a simple bullet agenda can be used if the meeting is more informational. The manager can chair the meeting but it's also reasonable to rotate the chairing of the meeting to give staff members experience at meeting management.

Decision-Making Meetings

Board or governance meetings of any kind usually involve making decisions for the organization. Planning and executing efficient decision-making meetings is greatly enhanced by knowing your priorities. The Action Agenda is an approach that brings great discipline to the process and that saves time and frustration that can characterize meetings that never seem to end or accomplish objectives.

The Action Agenda Makes Business Sense

A meeting called to make decisions is important. It differs from brown bag lunches, seminars, and the many other methods of building knowledge in the organization. It has to help you accomplish your ends or it wastes your time and delays important actions of the organization.

For many decades organizations large and small have used this business meeting model:

Old Business
New Business
Information

This approach leaves the manager of the meeting to be a benevolent dictator and make the meeting move along, but unless the manager is a great facilitator, old business tends to bog down the meeting so that new business is never discussed. Dysfunctional decision-making from the past comes back to haunt you again and again. Unresolved issues remain unresolved and become a barrier that keeps you from making progress. Old business is often "old" for a reason. It represents where you have been and not where you need to be now or where you need to go.

The action agenda is based on a simple but profound idea. Crafting the agenda carefully is the most important task. The agenda itself is a plan. It must be a plan to get decision-making done efficiently and with as much consensus as possible.

Send out a request for agenda items six weeks or more before the meeting. Ask all participants to submit any motions or discussion items in writing weeks before the event. Information items should be written and formatted for inclusion in a notebook or document with other meeting materials.

The three important categories in the "action agenda" business meeting are:

Action Items
Discussion Items
Information Items

These categories organize work in the meeting around priorities of the organization. The decisions about how to use the three categories are clear. You can place business items in the meeting by this simple process of triage:

Action Items

These items require a motion, the name of the motion maker, and an allotted amount of time for discussion before the decision. For example:

> *I move that we approve the memorandum of understanding with local government* (see attached document) by Jane Doe—thirty minutes.

This approach gives the decision making group a simple choice, to approve or disapprove of the motion after thirty minutes of discussion. Jane is the champion of the motion since she made it. Usually it works best to entertain discussion by having the motion maker explain it and then allow each person to comment on it round-robin style so that all participants have a chance to comment. A person can pass and then comment later after hearing the comments of others. A second round of comments can be entertained by the facilitator, if time permits. The time limit can be extended by consensus of the group but every effort should be made to keep the discussion within the time limit. If the motion fails, but discussion suggests a motion that might be approved, it can be made after voting down the first motion. Any document that supports the motion can be provided with the agenda and information items as an addendum.

All of the motions being presented in the Action Items category should be arranged in a priority order with the most important first and the least important last. There is a real sense of growing achievement in a business meeting that resolves its most important business decisions first and then works through them in an orderly way from most important to least important.

Discussion Items

These items involve discussions that could lead to a motion. They are built around important topics that the organization must consider, but they lack a clear mandate for which direction to go. Each should include a topic of discussion, a discussion leader, and a time limit. For example:

Camping Policy—Jim Johnson—fifteen minutes

Jim Johnson introduces the need for a camping policy for the organization but admits that no one has written a policy that is ready for consideration. The discussion allows each person to express a desire to see a policy developed or the belief that it is not needed or it is covered by some existing policy. The discussion might result in a motion to appoint a task force to develop a policy or it could simply end with agreement that no action needs to be taken. When no motion is made and time allotted elapses, you move on to the next discussion item. Discussion items should also be put in an order from the most compelling to the least.

Information Items

These items include the many details about the organization that need to be shared with the group, but do not require any decisions. They must be in writing and should be put in the board or committee notebook behind the agenda. They can be read at the leisure of each member of the group, but are not presented orally. If they require some interpretation or discussion, they should have been put in the previous category. No time allotment is needed on an item because no discussion will occur. The sponsor or person who prepared the report is named on the written item in case you want further clarification.

Process Management
The meeting facilitator conducts the meeting under Robert's Rules of Order or some other similar agreed-upon meeting management policy. A timekeeper should be appointed to remind everyone on the limits set per item. The facilitator is too busy with meeting management to also watch the clock. A parliamentarian can be appointed to see that Robert's Rules are followed. You should determine the meeting length in the original agenda and quit when the time is up, whether one hour or six hours of meeting time has elapsed.

The Action Agenda transforms organizations that have dysfunctional meetings because it provides a system that encourages decision-making while keeping participation balanced to build consensus. Making up the agenda is critically important. It must adhere to the process or nothing will work as planned. Usually the chairperson or manager will develop it and get approval from each other to make sure it meets the needs of the group. It is also introduced and approved at the beginning of the meeting to allow additions and changes. Anyone may comment that an item should be moved up or down in the agenda based upon its perceived importance. Once the agenda is set, adhere to it until the end of the meeting.

This process allows you to save time in meetings while getting first things done first. It makes priority setting a key act at the beginning of the process. It also builds consensus and respects the work of each member of the group. It takes a little practice to implement but it makes advocates of all who work with it because it makes a clear difference in productivity.

Action Agenda Best Practices

- Ask for motions and discussion items to be submitted in writing two weeks or more before the meeting.

- Motions include the name of the maker and a time limit.

- Ask for information items to be submitted in writing for copying and distribution with meeting materials.

- Organize the agenda with motions first, as action items, showing the sponsor and time limitation.

- Place discussion items second with a sponsor's name and a time limitation.

- Place information items last as a list showing the print copies that will be provided with the meeting packet.

- At the beginning of the meeting invite changes in items and time limitations including additional items.

- Appoint a timekeeper to monitor the progress on each item.

- Appoint a parliamentarian unless one already exists by protocol.

- Get input from each member of the group by using round-robin participation.

- Start the round-robin comments in a different location each time to create a democratic dynamic about who speaks first and last.

- Conduct the entire meeting within the original time limitation set for it. Adjourn on time even if all items are not completed.

- If your committee or board members use the Internet routinely, you may wish to post the agenda and information items on your Web site for participants to download in advance of the meeting.

4

Program Development

Experience Economy

Think about the last time you went to an interpretive site as a visitor. Maybe you took your family to the zoo or local nature center, or you went on an extended camping trip through a number of national parks. What aspects of the visit were the most memorable? If the experience was a positive one, chances are the answer to the question is something like, "We liked everything about it." If the experience was not positive, at what point did it go wrong? Often, it takes only one frustration to make you look at everything that happens from then on with a jaundiced eye.

Visitors are becoming more discriminating in the ways they spend their money and time. They seek experiences that will give them the best value for the hours or dollars spent. Economics theorists Joseph Pine and James Gilmore identify today's world as an experience economy. They published their ideas in the *Harvard Business Review* in August 1998, and Pine et al followed up with a book titled *The Experience Economy* in 2000. They suggest that the United States has seen a shift over time from an agricultural economy to a manufacturing or industrial economy to a service economy and finally to today's experience economy.

They use the analogy of a birthday cake to explain this shift. In the agricultural economy, people tended to make a birthday cake from scratch, using ingredients they produced on their own farm or for which they had bartered other goods. In the manufacturing economy, prepackaged cake mixes replaced much of the work involved in baking a cake. The service economy brought us markets with bakery departments that could personalize a cake ready to take home in a box. The experience economy features a ready-made cake, but also includes the party, complete with balloons, gifts, party favors, and games. People pay more at each step for the added value of the service and planning components. The idea of providing complete experiences is nothing new for many interpretive venues, but understanding and applying the characteristics of the experience economy theory can help those who have not successfully employed it gain a new perspective on their program.

Concessions run by your facility or partnerships with commercial enterprises can extend the reach of your programs. In Austin, Texas, boat tours help people view evening bat flights.

Pine and Gilmore suggested that Experience Economy businesses share five common characteristics:

1) *Maximizing positive cues.* Create a great first impression and then maintain it with excellent site and facility maintenance, attitudes of personnel, and attention to detail.

2) *Minimizing negative cues.* Remove unsightly, non-working, or dangerous items from public view.

3) *Establishing a theme.* Create a sense of place by having a consistent message that pervades all aspects of site, facility, and interpretive media.

4) *Involving multiple senses.* Incorporate smells, sounds, tastes, and tactile experiences to reinforce the visual experience.

5) *Providing memorabilia.* Develop thematic souvenir items that will help visitors remember their experience long after they leave the site.

Creating complete, quality visitor experiences means paying attention to the details in every aspect of your operation.

Non-traditional tables can be used as outdoor classrooms or picnic areas at the Cheng Du breeding center for giant pandas in China.

ticket stub becomes a souvenir Fang Chuan near the Jilin unchun Tiger Reserve in China.

vehicles exhibit imagery associated with he site at Shavers Creek Nature Center in ennsylvania.

In Peru, Cusqueño weavers demonstrate their craft at the "factory outlet" where alpaca sweaters, scarves, and other goods are sold.

Although Pine and Gilmore's research was developed and applied initially to the corporate world (think about the experience at a Barnes & Noble bookstore with its café, reading nooks, and special events), these characteristics can help any interpretive venue make a more memorable and positive experience for visitors, enabling agencies to achieve their missions more effectively.

Program Planning

When talking about an interpretive site, there are two uses of the term "program." A program can be a single presentation or the larger overall program in which all interpretive media, sales, and activities are considered. For the purposes of this book, "program" refers to the big picture. To help reduce confusion, specific interpretive presentations will be referred to as such rather than as programs.

Planning the overall program at an interpretive site involves much more than allowing individual interpretive staff to decide what sorts of presentations they would like to give. Generally, a program will consist of both personal and non-personal media. Personal media includes such things as guided walks, tours, living history demonstrations, special events, theatre, outreach presentations, campfire presentations, and other similar events. Non-personal media includes exhibits, publications, signs, sales items, landscape features, sculptures, recorded auto or pedestrian tours, food items, playscapes, and a variety of other creative methods of delivering your message. Most sites will benefit from providing a balance of personal and non-personal media, but determining what the appropriate mix of media will be at any given site requires a thoughtful planning process, usually conducted by an interpretive planning specialist.

Interpretive Planning: The 5-M Model for Successful Planning Projects by Lisa Brochu describes the need to consider management, markets, message, and mechanics before determining what media might work best for any given situation. This approach is true whether you are attempting to plan a system-wide interpretive program or a single presentation or exhibit. Failure to consider management needs and operational resources often results in media that does little or nothing to further the mission of the organization. If a market analysis is ignored, the message is likely to miss its mark. Mechanics help define the visitor experience by examining how site, facilities, and interpretation work together to create design balance and physical spaces that function as well as look good. Each of these factors is critical to the success of planning the overall program. Leave any one of them out and the chances of wasting money and time are greatly increased. There is a difference between an interpretive program and an effective interpretive program. The difference lies in careful planning.

Interpretation and Environmental Education

Although interpretation and environmental education share commonalities, they are two different things. The most concise way to describe the difference is that interpretation is a technique, while environmental education refers to subject matter. Both rely on measurable objectives to determine effectiveness; however, environmental education is generally designed to work with a specific curriculum in a formal classroom setting, often augmented by a visit to an interpretive site or a classroom visit by an interpreter. Interpretive techniques can and probably should be employed when planning and delivering environmental education, whether in the classroom or at an interpretive site, to make the lessons more enjoyable, relevant, and lasting. The two terms are not mutually exclusive, but it is important to understand the differences if they are each to be used most effectively.

Program Evaluation

Many interpretive programs are planned and some are implemented. Few are evaluated meaningfully. Before a program can be evaluated, it must have benchmarks against which success can be measured. Frequently, interpretive programs are planned with no measurable objectives at all, or with objectives that measure only outputs. Although an output (20,000 people will attend campfire presentations this year) is a valid measure of how many people are using a particular venue, such a measure does little to tell us whether the program is actually accomplishing anything. Measuring outcomes and impacts (see Chapter 1) is a much more valuable tool.

Developing an evaluation process for the interpretive program requires the determination of what would be considered meaningful results. So the first step is deciding what information is relevant and how it will be used. Ideally, the interpretive master plan includes measurable objectives that will provide a framework for the types of information to be collected; however, it should not be considered a limiting factor on the types of information to be collected. New needs or desires of management may be identified between the completion of the interpretive plan and the evaluation phase, so the evaluation instrument should be flexible enough to accommodate changing management needs. Once the purpose of the evaluation is clear, an appropriate method for collecting the information can be determined.

In the case of personal presentations, evaluations of the interpreter by randomly selected visitors or supervisory staff can provide important feedback for improvement of the individual's performance and relevance of the thematic message. External evaluations should generally be paired with self-evaluations completed by the presenter for a more complete picture of the performance. Evaluation techniques for non-personal media may include indirect observation (watching, listening to, and recording reactions of visitors from a distance so that they are unaware they are being observed), entry/exit interview surveys, comment cards, and a variety of other methods. Which method is most appropriate for a given situation will depend on the desired outcome. These evaluation tools help managers and interpreters learn more about how visitors perceive and react to the interpretive media; however, there are other criteria that may also be important to employ.

Evaluating the interpretive program against the annual budget can help justify its existence in ensuing years. Using the "bottom line" as an indicator to show results from the interpretive program is one way to prove that interpretation makes a difference in managing the operational resources of the site. But perhaps more important is evaluating the interpretive program against successful mitigation of damage to heritage resources. One site in west Texas was able to show that an aggressive interpretive campaign made a significant difference in the amount of vandalism to rock art sites within a state park. Stating the evaluation criteria as objectives that measure outcomes and impacts takes a little more thought, but can yield powerful results. Yosemite National Park invested money into an interpretive program that helped create awareness of the park's bears and how to keep bears, campers, and property safe. As a result, fewer bears have to be relocated or euthanized.

An effective evaluation tool demonstrates the success of the interpretive program in terms of outputs, outcomes, and impacts so that managers can prove that interpretation makes a difference in helping the agency achieve its mission.

5

Marketing

What Marketing Means for Interpretive Sites

Marketing is a frightening term to many managers and interpreters, particularly those who work for government agencies. The word "marketing" often connotes crass commercialism and may even offend some who feel their site is "above" the need for marketing. But marketing is much more than promotion, although promotion is certainly a piece of it. Marketing really involves an understanding of what the product or experience is; who the internal and external audiences are that might be associated with the product in some way and what they need, desire, and are willing to pay for with time or dollars; how the product can be promoted and targeted to appeal to current and potential audiences; what pricing strategies might be most appropriate for the target audiences; what interpretive niche needs to be filled given surrounding competitive and complementary functions; how to create partnerships that turn competitive functions into complementary functions; and what the most appropriate placement of services might be given the target audiences.

By definition, interpretive sites have some sort of resource with which to work. For some, it's an outstanding natural feature such as the Grand Canyon. For others, it may be a place with historical significance like the Lincoln Memorial. For many, the resource may not have global or national significance, but may be something of real regional, state, or local importance. Regardless of what the resource is, traditional resource-based planning assumes that "if they build it (a visitor center, a museum, an exhibit, a sign), visitors will come" because the resource is intrinsically interesting enough that simply providing access will bring numbers through the door. But whether or not visitors come and how many is not the point, unless the sole purpose is to create income and collect gate fees. The bigger issue at stake is, "Do visitors understand, appreciate, and become stewards of the resource and advocates for the agency?" Taking a market-based planning approach that thoughtfully examines the considerations outlined in the previous paragraph is more likely to yield success.

Market Research

Gathering information that will lead to informed decisions about your interpretive approach can be accomplished in a number of ways. Surveys of current and potential visitors are popular tools, but if not carefully crafted, survey instruments can skew results and provide false perspectives that lead to faulty decision-making. If a survey is to be your primary research instrument, use an experienced and reputable firm that can develop a survey instrument that will give results with as little bias as possible. Even more important, heed the results even if they are not what you were hoping to discover. The purpose of doing market research is to test ideas. Going ahead with an idea that your research indicates is likely to fail is irresponsible, wasting time and money that could have been better spent developing a new idea that might actually achieve the desired outcomes.

Promotion of Programs, Products, and Services

You may develop the most exciting and interesting interpretive program known to mankind at your site, but if the visiting public doesn't know about it, it will surely fail. Understanding your target audiences will help identify the most effective ways to reach them. You may decide to target a specific age, ethnic, or income group, but if all your promotional efforts are carried out in ways that your target group is unlikely to use (for example, putting flyers for a presentation targeted to inner city youth on state park bulletin boards will likely not draw many individuals from the targeted audience). Advertising companies have learned that using only one type of media or location for promotion of any one event lessens the chance of successful market penetration. Generally, marketing specialists recommend using a combination of five to six different approaches for any one event. So a special event at your site might be advertised in the newspaper, on radio, on television, on posted flyers, or by giving away free tickets at complementary sites and at stores that sell the types of goods that people interested in your event would be likely to buy.

To assess what promotional pieces are the most effective at reaching your target audiences, find ways to code each piece so that you can track where people are finding out about your site and program. Color-coding free or discount tickets, adding a lettered or numbered department code to registration forms, or even asking audience members how they learned about your program can help you plan more effective means of reaching your audiences in the future.

Pricing

Understanding your target markets can help in setting price structures that are reasonable for your particular area. But determining a fair price for your program must be based on more than just what the market will bear. Look at overall operations and take into consideration whether your program needs to recover its own cost, provide an income stream to cover other operational

Case Study

Survey instruments are only as good as the questions asked and the method of collection. Although any information is usually better than no information, be aware that developing unbiased survey questions is a fine art, best left to someone with experience in doing so. One client asked me to develop a survey to test a program idea that would guide the further development of an entire site. The client wanted to believe the concept they had come up with was a sound one for the market segment they were trying to attract. When they saw the unbiased questions I had written for the survey of local business owners and managers of resource management agencies (their target markets), they insisted that I add questions they developed which would clearly give them the response they wanted. When the bias was pointed out, they agreed to allow me to ask my questions as well as theirs.

When the results came back, their fear was realized. The market segments they had targeted with specific programming indicated that the timing and content of the programming was of little interest because of the busy schedules these people kept. However, they did express an interest in using the site as a community park where their families could go for weekend programming, which is precisely the use that the client wanted to avoid.

The end result was a compromise between what management wanted and what the markets wanted, so that the media (program) choice and site development reflected both desires without damaging the resource. My understanding at this writing is that the facility is now providing programming for both segments successfully. Had they gone ahead with the bias of their original survey questions, planning and development could not have progressed with the same successful result.

—Lisa Brochu

expenses, or whether it will be subsidized by some other means.

Consider the concept of perceived value when determining prices. Poorly designed, photocopied brochures or maps that are handed out indiscriminately often end up as litter. Well-designed publications that cost a quarter or a dollar are generally kept as mementoes of the trip. The perception of value and expectation of return works in terms of entry fees as well. A nature camp held at Disney World may be able to charge a great deal more than a similar experience held at a local not-for-profit nature center. The difference has nothing to do with quality of programming. But people anticipate a higher cost when attending a theme park and are willing to pay for what they perceive to be the higher quality experience associated with a well-known name.

Your program may lend itself to combination event tickets—one ticket for everything at the site or combinations of activities that allow customization of the experience for every visitor. (Pictured: Bob Bullock State History Museum)

Social Marketing

In the early 1970s health care professionals began using marketing principles to sell social ideas, attitudes, and behaviors. Environmental educators and interpreters have adapted the social marketing concept to encourage stewardship of natural and cultural resources. The social marketing model describes how interpreters hope to influence attitudes, beliefs and behaviors.

People who visit non-formal natural and cultural history sites usually are curious about the experience or may even be dragged along by a family member or friend. They may not have any awareness of the vulnerability of the resources or understanding of how their use of the area might harm the resources. Goals and objectives for interpretive programming usually include helping people connect with resources and become interested in being stewards. The leap from curiosity or being dragged along to active stewardship is a major change. The process takes time, many experiences with the resources, and considerable growth in knowledge and understanding. This transformation from curiosity to understanding to caring about the resource as stewards can be described as the interpretive opportunity continuum.

Good interpretation can help minimize potential conflicts or danger to humans and wildlife in outdoor settings by encouraging people to make better choices and develop a stewardship ethic.

The ultimate in interpretive management—just don't allow anything. Think about positive ways to encourage the right behaviors instead of more warnings signs.

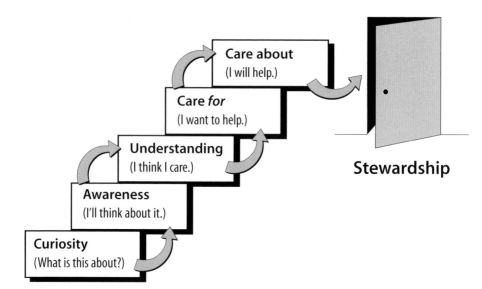

Depicted as a stair step process, this social marketing construct suggests strategies for helping people connect to the resource. Interpretive programming promotes awareness and increases the guest's knowledge of the resource. Interpreters can design opportunities for visitors to participate in stewardship activities such as beach cleanups or bird counts. Objectives can measure the increased commitment from participants. Maria Elena Muriel, a Certified Interpretive Trainer in Cabo San Lucas, Mexico, conducts turtle programs with an objective that "fifty percent of the audience will return after the program and help clean up the beach." If she asks before her talk who wants to do that, only a few are willing. Her inspirational interpretive presentation engages people and helps them understand why removing plastic bags from the beach may save the lives of sea turtles who eat them thinking they are jellies. She usually attains or exceeds her objective of fifty percent. Over time, this level of commitment has a real impact on the sea turtles.

Both marketing and social marketing rely on a willingness to try to understand audiences through observation, surveys, and what they select or buy as part of their experience. They come to interpretive sites with diverse attitudes, beliefs, and interests. As understanding of the audience grows, interpretive managers can better design programs, set realistic objectives, and evaluate results, encouraging stewardship over time. Most organizational missions focus on conservation, stewardship, protection of the resource, and related behaviors. In 1914 Secretary of the Interior Franklin Lane said to NPS Director Stephen Mather, "I'm looking for a new kind of public official, one who will go out in the field and sell the public on conservation." Social marketing provides the interpretive manager with a conceptual model for making a significant difference in the relationship of the visitor to the resource.

6

Policy and Procedures

The Three Sectors

Interpretation, like many other professions, is found in all three sectors, private for-profit, governmental, and not-for-profit. Government agencies employ the most interpreters and interpretive managers. The National Park Service is the largest single agency employer with about almost 4,000 full-time and seasonal field interpreters. This is a substantial percentage of the 20,000 full-time interpreters in the U.S., according to the National Association for Interpretation. Government interpreters may have working titles of park ranger, information specialist, guide, or even biologist. Many science-based positions include interpretive and outreach responsibilities.

In the private, for-profit business sector many interpreters work as guides with tour companies, cruise directors with cruise companies, or concessionaires who provide interpretive services at government properties. Not-for-profits have many interpreters at parks, zoos, nature centers, aquariums, and historic sites working in educational departments and outreach or interpretive programs. Each sector takes a somewhat different approach to policy and procedures,.

Government

Government agencies are generally created through enabling legislation. For example, the National Park Service (NPS) began with this landmark law in 1872, as described on the NPS Web site:

> The Yellowstone Act preserves the watershed of the Yellowstone River "for the benefit and enjoyment of the people." For the first time, public lands were preserved for public enjoyment, to be administered by the federal government. Put under the "exclusive control of the Secretary of the Interior," the land was "reserved and withdrawn from settlement, occupancy, or sale under the laws of the United States, and dedicated and set apart as a public park or pleasuring-ground."

Enabling legislation identifies the ultimate authority for the new park as the Secretary of the Interior. The National Park Service Organic Act in 1916 created the NPS as a full-fledged organization under the supervision of a director with the "fundamental purpose to conserve the scenery and the natural and historic objects and the wild life therein and to provide for the enjoyment for the same in such manner and by such means as will leave them unimpaired for the enjoyment of future generations." Additional acts of Congress in 1970 and 1978 further clarified the scope of authority of the leaders and managers of NPS.

It is important to know the enabling legislation behind your organization to understand the policy creation process. This process varies from agency to agency. Usually procedures are developed as a practical matter at a variety of levels from the director down to the managers and supervisory personnel. Procedures are simply the protocols or rules for how to handle business. They must align with the policies created at upper levels if the government agency is large. Your responsibility as a manager is to apply those policies through the application of procedures that help staff understand their roles and pursue them consistently. Someone else may create the policy but you interpret it and make it operational.

Some laws apply across agency boundaries, such as the Endangered Species Act or the National Environmental Policies Act (NEPA). U.S. Department of Labor and state labor laws govern private, public, and not-for-profit sectors alike. State and local government agencies must know which federal laws apply to them and which state or regional ones are relevant. Policy developed by the agency must be lawful and align with the legislation that created the organizations. Procedures make the policies operational, giving the front-line staff a clear idea of what is allowed and prohibited.

For Profit

For-profit businesses must obviously comply with Department of Labor laws as well as relevant environmental laws. Managers in this sector must know business law, internal revenue service statutes, and have the appropriate permits that provide access to the specific resources they interpret. Often this involves a license or access permit with a federal or state agency. Sometimes they gain access by virtue of a contract to provide specific interpretive services and they must comply with the guidelines in the contract or risk losing access. The contract defines their roles in representation of the agency.

Transportation of customers or clients becomes an important issue to research as well. Buses or vans that carry more than fifteen persons require Public Utilities Commission (P.U.C.) licenses and appropriate markings on the vehicles that identify the license number. Fifteen-passenger vans and smaller vehicles are often used for touring or transportation because of that requirement.

Do not rely on this book or any other similar resource as a final authority on transportation, IRS law, or any other regulation. Seek legal counsel or Certified Public Accountant assistance when you need specific guidance regarding legal licenses or reporting. Your state's labor department, unemployment program, workmen's compensation office, department of revenue and local taxing offices are all potential regulators of your activities. Be sure you know the specific laws in your geographic area so that your policies and procedures are compatible with the local regulatory environment.

Not-for-Profit

Not-for-profit organizations must comply with the same private sector laws as for-profit businesses. The Internal Revenue Service (IRS) requires that Form 990 be filed each year by May 15, but two extensions of three months each can be allowed by application. Often a time extension becomes necessary if you must wait for your Certified Public Accountant (CPA) auditor to complete your annual audit. Such an audit is recommended but not required by law. In addition to providing an objective review of the books for the board's comfort, government or foundation grant proposals often ask for an external audit along with a Form 990. Many CPAs give not-for-profits a better price if they wait until the May 15 filing deadline for private corporations is past.

You may also have to file a Form 990-T if you conduct business activities unrelated to your not-for-profit purpose. This form determines whether you will pay Unrelated Business Income Tax (UBIT) on the activity. UBIT is often owed for rental of building space, sale of ads, and other activities unrelated to your mission.

Not-for-profits, like government agencies, operate in an area of public trust and are rightly expected to behave ethically. Many not-for-profit organizations have a code of ethics statement that spells out their policies in procurement of goods and services, treatment of clients, and related behaviors. It identifies for board members, staff, and customers the boundaries or propriety in business and program dealings. Many professional organizations such as the National Association for Interpretation and the American Association of Museums have sample documents available on request.

Legalities

If you are a government manager negotiating a contract for interpretive services with a for-profit manager, you may need to know the contractor's legal environment as well as your own. Contractors have a profit motive and the contract has to respect that need while protecting the resource and agency interests. However, as a government representative you have a right to stipulate that the interpretive contractor be familiar with your mission, goals, and objectives. The contractor represents your agency to the public and should do so in the best possible manner. You should set the standards for the training of their personnel, especially with regards to interpretation. The public does not make the distinction between contractor and agency and will blame you if their product or service is inferior, dishonest, or in conflict with best practices related to the resource.

World War II President Harry Truman said, "The buck stops here." It was his way of accepting responsibility for his role as President of the United States. He didn't make excuses when things went wrong. We need a similar philosophy as managers within our own span of control. Making excuses to the public or blaming the boss sounds unprofessional and misses the point. We are managing the organization and everyone below us and above us is expecting legal, ethical and responsible behavior. We are the legal experts for our organizations at the site level in most cases. Our education about the law has to be continual because laws change and the court precedents are dynamic.

As an interpretive site manager, you have more than program management in your hands. You must be responsible for guest safety along with providing quality interpretive programming. Lawsuits for illegal or negligent behavior can and will often name a specific manager as well as the agency. The attorney of an aggrieved guest will name all entities who might reasonably have been expected to behave lawfully or with the best interests of guest safety in mind.

Documentation

Most of us cannot begin to carry all of the policies and procedures of our organization in our heads. We need a place to look it up. You can document important policies and procedures in manuals that can be available in staff break rooms or offices. They can also be put on a Web site so that volunteers, staff members, and concessionaires can download them as PDF files. Several of the more common kinds of manuals developed for these purposes are:

Emergency Procedures. Accident reports, insurance reports, and organizational notification protocols

Legal Postings. Department of Labor–required postings, workmen's compensation postings, sexual harassment procedures, etc. (visually displayed in employee access areas)

Operations Manual. Tax exemption letter, travel policy, report formats, etc.

Volunteer Manual. Rules, forms, inspirational messages, program ideas

Program Manual. Thematic program ideas, content bibliography, interpretive fundamentals, resource lists, form letters, etc.

Planning Manual. Plans, implementation procedures, guidelines, partner contact information, etc.

Code of Ethics. Statement of organizational ethical values, code of ethics pledge form

Consistency cannot happen if everyone must remember organizational policies and procedures without reminders. Manuals provide a handy way to "look it up." Be sure they are kept in print, available, and updated as needed so that everyone has the same information. These manuals can be given out during orientation and explained to new employees and volunteers. If they are critical policies with legal implications such as sexual harassment policy, personnel policy, and the like it may be required that they be posted in an appropriate public location. Many organizations sell posters that meet state and federal posting requirements and these are usually cost effective ways to stay legal.

When policies refer to the termination of employees or release of volunteers, provide a cover sheet that must be signed. This procedure documents that each person subject to the policy has had the opportunity to read the manual or policy, keeping someone from saying later that he or she didn't know about the policy. Documentation of this kind becomes very important if firing an employee or dealing with a specific grievance. With volunteers it simply provides clarity and lessens hard feelings if they must be released because their behavior violates critical policies or compromises the quality of your work with guests. They represent you and must be evaluated similar to employees.

Record Keeping

The following provides a brief description of some recommended record keeping methods.

Double-Entry Bookkeeping

This traditional method of tracking business financial matters involves two kinds of reports—income and expense (I/E) report and the balance sheet. The I/E report lets you know on a monthly, quarterly, and annual basis whether your organization is profitable or not. Some call it a profit and loss report. The balance sheet shows changes in assets owned by the organization along with liabilities or debts against the assets. Ideally the balance sheet shows a net increase in assets each year because your I/E report indicates you made a profit or surplus. Private sector organizations routinely use this system while governmental bookkeeping is often specific to the agency or governmental unit.

Programmatic Time Keeping

You can keep employee time records very simply with number of hours worked each day and a special symbol when sick or vacation time is used. However, programmatic time keeping requires each employee to record time daily in a variety of program and facility categories. This approach allows you to analyze how employees spend their time and project future needs for labor in specific areas. The Internal Revenue Service especially encourages this approach because it shows your commitment to mission-based programs. It tracks the commitment of human resources to the stated purpose of the organization. Your auditor will use it to allocate expenditures to either programs or administration which is evaluated during IRS audits. Foundations also have an interest in the allocation of funds to program versus administrative needs. Usually it is expected that eighty percent or more of income is committed to programs.

Program Calendar

This schedule can be kept on a computer, an old-fashioned calendar, or one of those visual wall calendars that allow all to see what is scheduled from a distance. It should be sufficiently detailed to allow anyone to quickly identify what groups will come to the site, what programs they expect, and who is responsible for those. The calendar is a practical tool but the documentation it provides may also be evaluated during an IRS audit to see whom you serve and how you serve them. Keep these records at least three years in a well-labeled storage box.

Indemnification Releases

Releases are the legal forms you may ask customers to sign at any facility when renting a bicycle, on a canoe, allowing access to back country or whatever. When customers sign release forms, they acknowledge that they know the activity is potentially dangerous and will "hold harmless" the organization and any cosponsors providing the products or services. These waivers do not protect you from being sued but they may cause guests to pause before suing because they know they have acknowledged the danger. In court your insurance company will be glad you have developed and saved these records. They can be essential in making the case that the client understood the potential for accidents. Store them for at least three years in a well-labeled storage box.

Legal Records and Reports

Nothing will give you more heartburn than to discover you are behind with state or federal agencies on required reports. They usually have stiff penalties for not filing so it is best to file these in a timely manner. Keep a calendar with reminders of these required reports in a visible location in your office.

Policies, procedures, and reports are a fact of life in management. As an individual, you may be disorganized and slovenly. As a manager, your attention to detail must be exact. Employers expect it, the law requires it, and your reputation is easily undone if you make serious mistakes. Seminars are offered by local government, not-for-profit help agencies, and private sector trainers to build your skills in these areas. They are worth the cost, time, and effort to stay up on the law, your organizational requirements and trends in the legal environment. You are less likely to need an attorney if you stay in touch with the evolving legal environment of business and changes in organizational policies.

Record or Report	Description	Timing
IRS 941 Report	FICA and Federal tax withheld	Quarterly
IRS 940 Report (FUTA)	End-of-year 941 reconciliation plus Federal Unemployment Taxes (FUTA)	Annual—not-for-profits are FUTA-exempt
State Tax Report	State taxes withheld	Quarterly (usually)
Tax Deposits	Funds deposited at your bank for taxes due	Varies with size of business—consult your accountant
SUTA	State unemployment taxes withheld	Required in most states
Workmen's Comp Report	wages for which workmen's compensation taxes must be paid	Quarterly in most states
Sales Tax Reports	Sales taxes due to the state and local government	Quarterly in most states
IRS 990 & 990-T	Not-for-profit income tax reports—990-T—Unrelated Business Income Tax (UBIT)	Annually, May 15 deadline
Private Personal and Corporate IRS Forms	Form numbers vary with type of business, sole proprietor, or corporate	Consult your tax advisor for dates required to file each specific form

Legal records and reports

Operations

Operations will manage you unless you plan properly and manage them. It is easy to become a reactive manager who simply runs from crisis to crisis, never figuring out exactly why that spare time to catch up and plan never happens. The following areas are some of the many balls you must juggle as a successful manager.

Inventories

Accounting for the "stuff" you manage is more than making lists on a database. Inventories have a variety of values in the business and program areas of the organization.

Sales Inventory

One of the more important inventories for not-for-profit and for-profit organizations is the inventory of sales items. This inventory is required by Internal Revenue Service law and should be done at the end of the year. It is important that this be very accurate and kept in a form that multiplies the quantity of each item times the wholesale value to determine the asset value of each item in your books. This inventory goes on your balance sheet as an asset. If you have a store, program sales, mail-order sales, or any other kind of vendor activity, this end-of-year inventory must be done and will be double-checked by your auditor if you have an external audit done. You have spent money to create this inventory so it shows up as an asset on your balance sheet, which recognizes your investment in a way that will make sense to those evaluating your net worth as an organization.

Equipment Inventory

Another legal inventory that is important is the list of capital equipment items your organization owns. Usually your accountant will keep this list for you but it's wise to review it with them annually to remove items taken out of service, sold to recover value, or given away to other organizations. Most equipment items are depreciated on three- to seven-year schedules and equipment items that are not

A simple, direct approach may get the message across, or may not. Without further explanation, it is unclear whether rattlesnakes are dangerous, desirable, in their natural setting, or fair game.

Then again, even explanations don't always get the job done. When serious danger may be present, a staff person or volunteer may be necessary to warn and monitor visitors.

very lasting or useful will often be taken out of service before being depreciated and should be taken off the asset inventory. Equipment should also be labeled with a number or identifying code so that similar items of different ages can be recognized easily for warranty or related purposes. The depreciated value of these assets also shows up on your balance sheet as a positive figure, recognizing your investment and adding to your net worth.

Resource Inventory

Lists or databases of natural and cultural artifacts can be kept in a variety of ways and for a variety of reasons. When planning new exhibits, programs, and facilities, it is valuable to know what kinds and quantities of items you need to store and protect. Conservancy of cultural artifacts can be quite costly and might require special expertise. The Institute of Museum and Library Services, a branch of the U.S. Government, has grants to assist with these kinds of curatorial activities. You may have to create a conservation program for very valuable paintings, documents, or artifacts to properly protect them. They must be labeled clearly with a number or code and relevant data about them (where found, when found, etc.) should be

TIM MERRIMAN

Security may involve electronic devices, human resources, or a combination of systems. Security personnel can help promote the mission of the site if trained in customer service and interpretation. (Pictured: Smithsonian Institute)

recorded in your database inventory for them.

Species inventories of natural areas are valuable in establishing a baseline for the property to evaluate resource management over a period of time. If you have 650 species of plants on a natural area or park when the first inventory is done and 625 a decade later, you need to discover what is causing the decline in biodiversity on the property. Often you can get botany and zoology departments at nearby universities to help conduct a site inventory by bringing taxonomy classes to your area. Studies that show plant frequency and vegetation zones take more time, but a simple species inventory is a start. Annual Audubon Christmas Counts are easy to sponsor and a terrific way to monitor wintering birds each year.

Sustainability programs being developed around the world are invariably built on having good data about changes in the quantities and quality of plant and animal populations. Some organizations have regular "bioblitzes" that bring volunteers out to inventory all of the plants and animals on an area at the same time each year. This technique provides a way to evaluate your natural resources inexpensively. As the "blitz" is repeated you can spot declines in populations and consider conservation measures. The data will also help not-for-profit organizations land grants to assist with efforts to prevent further population declines.

Other Inventories
Other useful inventories might include databases or lists of books, music recordings, photos, rocks, minerals, record-sized trees, archaeological sites, and cemeteries. You may find that knowledge of old cemeteries on your properties will endear you to visitors who do genealogical research. Plotting locations of specific resources or concentrations of resources on a site map can reveal the potential for areas you might want to steer visitors to or encourage them to avoid through careful site planning. Web sites provide an easy way to share the various inventories of resources you collect with audiences. Bird or wildflower checklists are very popular ways of sharing your inventory knowledge with specific user groups. Photo inventories are extremely helpful when the time comes to develop publications, signs, or exhibits. A good inventory of available images can save hundreds or thousands of dollars that might otherwise be spent to illustrate non-personal media.

Buildings
Management of buildings and engineered facilities is an important responsibility. They demand maintenance at a level that protects their value to the organization and provides guests with a safe experience. Local, regional, and state statutes dictate some of the rules. Managers must know the fire codes, building permit procedures, and other legal requirements. Food preparation facilities are the most complicated because public health laws are some of the most stringent regulations and inspections tend to be frequent and thorough in most areas.

Maintenance plans need not be lengthy or complex but can simply be a checklist and calendar that reminds staff when regular maintenance activities will happen. Ideally, you will have a maintenance staff that takes pride in care of buildings and grounds, but smaller organizations must sometimes draw on every staff member to contribute to maintenance. The care of buildings speaks loudly about values of the organization. Litter, smudgy windows, unswept hallways, and flaking painted surfaces tell the guest that your concern about quality is low. They will wonder if that extends to interpreting to their children or care of items they donate. Send the message that details matter. Take care to maintain all buildings and facilities at a high level.

Public safety is also in your hands. Neglecting a broken handrail, ice on stairs, or other public hazard can lead to serious injuries and certainly encourages lawsuits. Unrepaired vandalism has been proven to attract more vandalism. Remove damage to property as soon as it is seen and you save yourself work.

Insurance
Evaluate insurance for buildings, facilities, programs, and general liability annually.

As you grow as an organization, your insurance limits need to increase and new coverages may be advisable. Be sure that your insurance salesperson actually visits your site occasionally to look at operations and ask you questions. A major loss from a flood, fire, or utility failure may look more like a management failure. You need to be able to reassure your governance group and staff that you have the appropriate coverage that will allow you to replace facilities lost to unforeseen catastrophes. Accidents will happen and you need to be prepared.

Liability insurance for staff and the board of trustees is always a good idea. Some state laws indemnify the boards of not-for-profit organizations from personal liability. However, in the event of a lawsuit you want the attorney from your insurance company addressing the issue. A board member might be sued, fight the suit, and win but spend a small fortune on the event. It should be the organization that protects staff, board members, and volunteers from litigation costs.

Landscape

The landscaping, paths, outdoor facilities, and water features of a property create a rich backdrop for interpretive programs. They should support the central theme of the property in design and be functional, friendly, and well-maintained. A landscape architect may be hired by a for-profit organization but might work for free for a not-for-profit. Government organizations sometimes employ landscape architects or hire them on contract. They are skilled at determining drainage, irrigation, and traffic flows while improving the look and thematic style of the property. To get the best possible approach to landscaping, hire or solicit landscape architecture services from someone who understands your kind of interpretive organization. You may want and need water-efficient xeriscape plants to tell your guests that you care about water conservation. A golf course landscape architect may not share that sensitivity to water conservation issues. You can locate specialized services like this through NAI's *Green Pages*, but be sure to ask bidders for references. Call those for whom they have worked recently and ask about their skills and sensitivity to interpretive issues.

Landscape maintenance is absolutely paramount for botanic gardens, and arboretums. Parks, natural areas, and nature centers often rely on natural landscapes to provide ambiance, so they tend to avoid installing turf, formal gardens, or labor-intensive plantings. Native landscape plantings are valuable as teaching resources and usually require less care, fertilization, and insect control. They are well-adapted to local soils, rainfall, and insect populations. They usually match up to your theme most easily.

There are exceptions, however. A historic home of the 1840s might need a landscape plan that is locked in that era with a formal rose garden or other plantings of old varieties of horticultural plants. They help set the scene and create the backdrop for interpreting cultural history.

Five or more signs that say the same thing still don't guarantee that visitors will understand the message. A more effective (and less expensive) approach might be one well-designed sign.

Plan trail and building surfaces with an eye to future maintenance and accessibility issues.

Let the visiting public in on your plans. At best, you'll find hidden support; at least, you may encourage repeat visits.

TIM MERRIMAN

Coming Soon...

We are building a trail to interpret the effects of fire on the High Desert.

Please come back to walk this new path in the spring!

WIND, EARTH, AND FIRE INTERPRETIVE TRAIL

The High Desert forest that surrounds you tells a fascinating story. If you look closely, the landscape will reveal both its history and its possible future, and how natural and man-made forces including fire have shaped it.

Blending management messages with interpretation makes more of an impact and may provoke further thought or action on the part of the visitor.

LISA BROCHU

DESERT SWAMP

Poorly maintained grounds and interpretive signs send the message that the quality of your visitors' experiences doesn't matter.

Exhibits

Exhibits are valuable media for telling interpretive stories. Hopefully you have chosen to have exhibits as the result of a careful interpretive planning process. Not every interpretive facility needs them and exhibits have the most impact when they are well-designed and placed to accomplish specific objectives with identified audiences. Exhibits and exhibit areas should not be an end to themselves.

Interpretive planners who are well-trained know that exhibits should be designed to achieve mission-related objectives, while helping connect thematic messages with specific audiences. Great exhibits are usually the result of careful design that effectively conveys ideas or messages to the audience in a creative way that works. They are usually best when planned collaboratively with planners, researchers, designers and fabricators.

Exhibits also require maintenance. Broken or malfunctioning exhibits labeled with a "BROKEN" sign tell the guest you do not value your own messages or their experience. Exhibits must be checked on a regular schedule. Repair damage immediately or get the exhibit out of the public's view.

Exhibits are rarely intended to be left where they are and as they are forever. They should be refurbished on a schedule even if timeless in how they interpret. Updating them, replacing them, and rotating some of them seasonally are all ways of making an exhibit area more dynamic. If you want return visits to your site, your audiences must think of your interpretive facilities as being exciting and ever-changing. Otherwise they will feel they have "been there and done that."

The Monterey Bay Aquarium uses a three-year exhibit rotation cycle for major exhibit changes. As soon as a new exhibit is installed, planning begins on the next exhibit, allowing three years for a thorough job of planning, design, testing, construction, and installation. Because the aquarium uses live animals with specific requirements for their habitat exhibits, some exhibits are "regulars" that visitors count on seeing every time they come to the aquarium, but with a high percentage of repeat visitors, the attention to rotating other exhibits creates constant interest in returning.

Program Materials

Collections at interpretive sites often include one-of-a-kind artifacts and natural items that cannot easily be replaced. These collections should be preserved and protected in exhibit cases or stored properly. Collections of materials that can be handled are sometimes described as teaching collections because they have value as educational or interpretive items. They can take the wear and tear of being used by children and adults to understand ideas, but eventually they will wear out or become damaged and need replacement. Durable replicas work well in teaching collections.

Skulls, nests, food items, casts of tracks, and scat are especially interesting in animal programs. Most of these items are now available as realistic replicas cast in various kinds of plastic. The replicas last longer and look just like the original

Case Study

While managing the Greenway and Nature Center of Pueblo in Colorado, I found that we simply lacked the funds to properly care for our sixty acres. Since we could afford only one full-time staff member for grounds maintenance, we hired a person with the human resource skills to manage others, specifically court-assigned community service workers. We became well-acquainted with the counselors in the local juvenile judicial programs. Juveniles and nonviolent offenders were assigned to do from forty to several hundred hours of work for us. Our grounds superintendent assigned and supervised the maintenance work, coached the workers, and reported back to the judicial system. It worked well for us in that community. Those with community service hours to invest enjoyed working in our unique natural setting and we liked helping young people get an experience with the outdoors that might alter their attitudes about personal property protection. Often they were assigned to fix something after creating similar damage somewhere else. The lesson is learned more often through this kind of restitution.

Near our buildings and intensively used areas we wanted more formally planted landscaped areas with native plants, including xeriscape demonstrations. We found that families were very willing to sponsor a garden area in memory of a deceased loved one, so we funded these landscaping improvements with memorial donations. The impact was great for we transformed our high-use areas into demonstration gardens with native plants. It was wonderful to watch families bring their loved ones out to see the gardens in memory of a special person. Because the designs were natural and used native plants, the gardens became teaching collections for children on field trips.

On a recent visit to the Greenway and Nature Center, a man in his early thirties said hello to me by name. "You may not remember me, but I was one of the community service workers here as a teenager. This is my six-year old son and we came out to go fishing. We love this place." Our investment in helping connect people of all ages with the resource is handsomely rewarded when someone reminds us of how they got involved. And this man is teaching his child about the Earth and the nature center because he had an experience with us that mattered very much.

—Tim Merriman

materials. Many exhibit fabrication studios can make plants and animals out of artificial materials that look very much like the real things. It's important to tell people that the things they are seeing or touching are replicas, particularly when showing reproductions of historic artifacts.

Make sure that the experience of the visitor matches the message you think you're sending. If conservation matters at your site, provide recycling bins to reinforce the message.

Live Animals

The display of living animals is a big responsibility. If you are trying to teach people respect for animals, they must see that respect reflected in every nuance of your care for captive animals. Many nature centers and zoos use rehabilitated animals that cannot be released for programs. It adds value to explain that the eagle cannot fly due to injuries from electrical lines. Not keeping otherwise healthy wild animals as pets becomes part of the message.

If you plan to use or display live animals of any kind, develop a clear set of policies and procedures that let staff and volunteers know what the handling, care, display, and program uses of live animals will be. Make sure all staff and volunteers are telling the same story regarding the reasons for keeping and exhibiting live animals. The public expects your treatment of animals to be humane and thoughtful. They may even ask to see the policies regarding their handling.

Maintenance and housing of animals must meet reasonable standards. Do not keep animals if you lack the funds to keep and care for them properly. Volunteers will often enjoy being involved in the husbandry activities, but must have appropriate training in procedures and proper protection equipment.

TIM MERRIMAN

A "bamboo" fence made of durable materials cuts down on maintenance and reinforces the overall experience at Sichuan Province's Panda Research and Breeding Center in Cheng Du.

Liability is an important consideration. Staff must be comfortable that a snake or turtle can tolerate being touched in a program without becoming upset or trying to bite. No matter how tame an individual animal might be, the public should not handle some kinds of animals. A tame squirrel at a nature center being touched or petted could encourage children to try to catch or touch a wild squirrel in their neighborhood. That encounter will likely result in injuries and you may be blamed for setting the example.

Handling or touching the tamest animals, such as box turtles, should include a good hand-washing lesson. Some zoo programs use moist towelettes with an anti-bacterial agent after programs in which people handle live animals. If you offer the opportunity to touch any animal, provide a hand-washing station immediately adjacent to the exhibit or program area.

Equipment

Maintenance and storage of equipment is also an important responsibility. These items are valuable assets of the organization and as such, many items may need locked areas to protect them. As your staff grows in number, you may need a

Income	
Ads—Newsletter	$2,000
Annual Campaign/Donations	$35,000
Grants—Operating	$40,000
Memberships	$220,000
Miscellaneous	$1,000
Rentals—Recreation Equipment	$5,000
Sales—Gift Shop	$45,000
Special Events	$90,000
TOTAL INCOME	**$438,000**
COST OF SALES	
Member Service Goods	$110,000
Sales Items	$25,000
TOTAL COST OF SALES	**$135,000**
NET INCOME	**$303,000**
Expenses	
Ads/Promotion	$1,000
Bad Checks/Debts	$50
Bank/Credit Card Charges	$1,000
Committees	$1,000
Contract Services	$5,000
Licenses and fees	$500
Miscellaneous	$500
Payroll/Payroll Expenses	$225,000
Postage	$15,000
Printing/Duplication	$8,000
Professional Fees	$4,000
Repairs/Maintenance	$5,000
Supplies	$10,000
Telecommunications	$6,000
Travel	$4,000
Utilities	$3,000
TOTAL EXPENSE	$289,050
Surplus	**$13,950**

Sample Budget for a Small Museum or Nature Center

checkout procedure to keep track of equipment. Often a staff of ten or more members will include a technician or equipment specialist who manages storage and maintenance, especially if you work with specialized items such as complex or expensive computers, projectors, electronic exhibits, and phone systems. You should also have a file drawer with a file for each piece of equipment that contains the operations manual, original invoice copy, warranty information, and serial number. If you have a theft, damage, or malfunction, these resources are needed to get repairs or replacements.

Your accountant or some other office should have a list of your equipment, values, and serial numbers in the event of a fire or other catastrophic damage. Your insurance claim will require a record of what was lost.

Budget Development and Tracking

Operating budgets vary widely, depending upon your sector. Government budgets are usually a plan for spending funds. They usually conform to a format required by your agency. Creativity in developing a budget system will not be rewarded. You are part of a larger system and must understand the budget approach and monitoring requirements at the start.

Many governmental agencies now allow interpretive operations to charge for some programs or services and they measure revenue recovery. They may not expect you to earn all of the funds being spent, but might compare you to other business units based upon percentage of expenses recovered through revenue programs. If your system works this way, you must be knowledgeable about other business divisions and how they perform. Improving your percentage of revenue recovered can be one of the objectives you measure each year.

Not-for-profit and for-profit budgets include income categories. Writing a first-year budget for a new operation is challenging because you have no certain idea of what the revenues or expenses will be. You develop a budget on a computer spreadsheet that you hope is realistic. Monitor it monthly to see how it performs in reality compared to your estimates. At the end of the first year you can write a budget that is more accurate, using the actual numbers from the previous year. Growth projections for income may be reasonable but you need to know that you have strategies in your marketing plans to create growth.

Too often a not-for-profit or for-profit organization relies on too few income categories. It is wise to diversify your sources of income so that a decline in one area is not a crisis. Having six or seven major income categories provides a cushion against economic recessions. Even interest income from invested funds in an endowment for a not-for-profit can be a problem in times when interest rates are down or the stock market is in retreat. Always plan your budget projections of income with a plan for what you do if revenues do not grow as planned.

Expenses in a budget are often recorded in a double-entry bookkeeping system in two locations. Overhead expenses that relate to fixed costs such as salaries, utilities, rent, and supplies are at the bottom of the budget as *expenses*.

TIM MERRIMAN

Provide a place for comments and complaints to allow visitors the opportunity to make a difference. Follow up promptly if at all possible.

"Cost of Goods or Services" related to purchase of materials or temporary services for resale are in a category between "Income" at the top and "Expenses" at the bottom. These fluctuate widely in relation to sales volumes. Your budget will show "Total Income" with "Costs of Goods or Services" deducted to give a "Gross Income" figure. Then the expenses are deducted to show net profit. If you have a food service, the food purchased or part-time wait staff might be in the "Costs of Goods or Services" category because they vary upward or downward wildly with sales volumes. In a bookstore the costs of purchasing inventory will often be in a "Cost of Goods" category.

Controlling spending is usually a matter of giving those with spending authority a budget and procedures for making expenditures. It works best when you give them an incentive for controlling spending. Some organizations give staff a percentage of surplus or profit as a bonus. This practice encourages all who expend funds to be careful when spending. Surplus is greatest when revenue is optimized and expenses are minimized. If there is no incentive to control expenses, you should not be surprised when staff spends all that was allowed in the budget. It is natural to want more "stuff" but we all become more frugal if we have a stake in being careful with spending.

8

Memorabilia

Somewhere on your walls, in a drawer, or on your desk is an item that you have only to glance at to evoke a smile that goes to the depths of your memories. Dr. Ed Mahoney at Michigan State University calls this a Post Marketing Icon (PMI). It's his name for souvenirs that have the power to recall a great experience. Ethan Rotman of California Fish and Game refers to most souvenirs as pre-trash (PT), items that clutter up our desk drawers, garages and closets only to become part of the waste stream of our lives. So what are memorabilia or souvenirs really? PMIs or PTs?

The answer is: they can be either or something in between. Some of what we buy or pick up at natural or cultural history sites are PTs. They will be a part of that magnificent collection of insignificant junk that follows us around until we condemn it to a garage sale, white elephant gift, or dumpster. But you cannot discount the power of a true PMI, a real icon that absolutely recalls an experience with dramatic power. Think of that photo you have, that ticket stub, that item that makes you smile or brings a tear to your eye because it evokes an entire experience you cherish or do not want to forget.

At a scholarship auction for the National Association for Interpretation, a very nice photo of Delicate Arch in Arches National Park from K.C. Publications sold for more than $600. When the buyer/donor was asked why he was willing to give that much for a photo, he said, "That was the first place I hiked with my only grandchild." He wanted it to recall an afternoon of incredible power in his life, the chance to share an outdoor experience with a grandson. He saw the photo and had to have it. It sold so high because another NAI member bid for it to the bitter end. She later said that she and her husband hiked to Delicate Arch one night and watched the moon set through the arch. She wanted to hang the photo as a reminder of that magical evening. Both of them liked the idea that the cost of this photo would support a scholarship for a student. This PMI would feel good several ways.

In Pine and Gilmore's "Experience Economy" article (1998), the authors say,

"People purchase memorabilia as tangible artifacts of experiences." We know that visitors and guests at natural and cultural sites will also create their own memorabilia. They take photos, draw pictures, and write poetry. Those are the wonderful things that can happen. They also pick up fossils, break off rocks with petroglyphs, dig up midden areas, and transplant rare plants as memorabilia. They sometimes destroy the resource out of the simple desire to have a PMI, memorabilia from a unique event or experience.

Rob Pacheco of Hawaii Forest & Trail indicates that his guests sometimes send back a piece of lava picked up on a hike. They read or hear about Madame Pelé, goddess of fire and volcanoes, who angers when her lava is taken. When they have a streak of bad luck, they decide to return the PMI just in case. We cannot expect guilt to work on our behalf in this way very often. And a small piece of lava rock from the world's largest volcano is probably a more sustainable piece of memorabilia than most other things taken from a natural site, if taken legally. You can buy lava gravel on the Big Island by the ton for a few dollars.

Historic sites have the challenge of conserving sites, buildings, and artifacts that will degrade even if the visitor does not take or abuse them. An artifact taken or damaged is tough to replace and we surely do not want folks taking a piece of the site or land. We have to think about this natural inclination to tangibilize memories and turn it in a positive direction.

Sometimes otherwise well-intentioned people may even kill or injure an animal to get a souvenir. Tide pool interpretation is especially problematic. When you turn your audience on to the mysteries and intrigue of a tide pool, they may sneak back to the pool to get a starfish without realizing what they're doing. The creature seems to be like a leaf, something that can be preserved easily, but they unwittingly kill the animal. Helping them create a reasonable souvenir from the experience may keep them from taking something precious.

Creating Memorabilia

Take the tide pool example. What could you create as a piece of memorabilia from that interpretive experience that would mean something to your guests? You might give them a beautiful piece of paper or card with a tracing or screened photo of a real starfish on it. Ask each of them to write a poem about the day, their feelings, the sanctity of life in the ocean. If the group seems to have bonded with each other, invite them to have their friends sign the card and date it as memorabilia. Think about the signatures in your high school yearbook that somehow capture the sweet naiveté of that moment in your life. These simple things can mean the most.

Encourage your staff to have a creative brainstorming session that will result in developing meaningful memorabilia for interpretive experiences at your site. Simply offering to take a photo with a guest's camera may be enough to help the guest recall the experience after returning home.

Hot air balloonists have created a tradition or ritual that happens at the

Case Study

The Whole Earth Nature School in Japan takes children and guests into an ice cave on Mount Fuji as part of its regular programming. It's a magical experience. On a recent visit, Masa Shintani led me on a crawl through a narrow slit at the bottom of a sinkhole over a vapor cave. We slid on our bottoms on ice for hundreds of yards looking at icy stalactites and stalagmites in the cave with the soft illumination of a headlamp. Then they turned out the lights and asked me to listen. I heard dripping. Masa explained that the guides tell children that the ice beneath them is 200 feet thick and water droplets take sixty-five years to travel through the ice and into the aquifer below. "You are sitting on the drinking water of your grandchildren," they reveal. It's powerful to think about the water percolating through lava rock to freeze in the cave, slowly migrating downward to become the drinking water of Tokyo. After the cave experience, they served me hot green tea and chocolate-covered almonds as we sat on the snow on a space blanket. Surrounded by the forest, they taught me that the Kanji symbols of the Japanese language tie back to the trees and natural world. The characters are drawings of nature, a powerful message about our relationship with the Earth. One of the Kanji symbols for the "nothing tree" (beech tree) became my souvenir of the experience. They explained that beechwood is used for nothing traditionally and it was called the nothing tree. If the nothing tree kanji had been drawn on a piece of paper made from beechwood, it would have been even more wonderful as a souvenir. The icicles in the cave were safe as icons. Since they melt, people don't take them. The lava rock is supposed to stay in the national park. I carry the Kanji symbols from that day with me and tell people I meet about the experience.

—Tim Merriman

closure of an experience. They use orange juice or champagne as refreshment while reading a poem or prayer that captures the beauty of the moment.

> The winds have welcomed you with softness
> The sun has blessed you with its warm hands
> You have flown so high and so well
> that God has joined you in your laughter
> and set you back again
> into the loving arms of mother earth

Some balloon companies also give out or sell a cloisonné pin or a patch with their logo. The memory of an experience does not require an expensive icon to recall it. The best icon will relate to the experience. A photo, postcard, or poem may get the job done. Signatures and personal remarks on the card or photo by group members can add to the value.

LISA BROCHU

Gift shops can be a valuable income stream and help promote the mission of your site, but only if the goods sold reflect the intended message, like that of the Dinosaur Center in Wyoming.

Look around your home and office. Do you have PMIs? They are everywhere in our lives. We wear rings to make tangible our wedding vows, hang our children's artwork on the fridge, and collect autographs when we meet a celebrity or author. Some of us pick up a T-shirt or cap at places we love because each wearing of the item becomes a reminder of a special experience. Memorabilia recall the experience. As managers of interpretive sites, we can facilitate the provision of memorabilia that help people remember our messages as part of the experience they've had at our sites.

As for the PTs—the pre-trash—avoid the tendency to buy fabricated items that do not really connect with the experience for your sales racks. Think about how you create emotional connections and use the icons to recall that. Help people understand that a live starfish, a rare fossil, or a native orchid is not the right thing to remind them of the experience because taking it would diminish the resource. Suggest something even better—propagated orchids that can be planted at home, replica fossils, or starfish artwork. In Africa beautiful notecards made from processed elephant dung stimulate folks to show their friends this unique product. An added benefit is that some of the

TIM MERRIMAN

Redesigning enclosures for pandas at Wolong Panda Breeding Center in China solved a management problem created by tourists wanting close-up photographs of the animals.

profit goes to support the native people who make the cards and preserve habitat of the elephants.

Some of the more traditional items such as souvenirs, T-shirts, sweatshirts, mugs, charms, spoons, shot glasses, and the like fall somewhere in the middle of the spectrum of thematic memorabilia, depending on the message, if any, that they communicate. Some folks will buy them as treasured items in a collection of memorabilia from trips. But rubber spiders, plastic tomahawks, and artifacts mass-produced half-way around the world from the location being remembered or that have no reasonable relationship with the experience at the site would best be omitted from your sales offerings. They do little to enhance the experience and tend to become trash quickly instead of a treasured PMI.

Retail Operations

The sale of items related to an interpretive site can be a great addition to the experience or a great distraction. Following the line of reasoning about PMIs and PTs, you can sell things with great potential as PMIs (post marketing icons) or educational tools and you have enhanced the experience. If you are simply selling

Case Study

I had traveled to Oregon with my sons, then 13 and 9, to take a week-long trip through the state. At one museum we encountered a fascinating beadwork exhibit kept us occupied for the better part of an hour. The exhibit was simple—amid examples of beadwork from native people throughout the area was an enlarged bead loom with chunky wooden beads in a box. A diagram indicated how simple it was to begin stringing beads and creating designs. The exhibit included stools for each of three stations so we immediately sat down and got to work. It was creative, fun, engaging, and stimulated a new respect for the handiwork of the cultures with which we becoming familiar. Sharing this experience with my sons made it a highlight of the trip. When we made our way to the gift shop, I asked about beading supplies and books and was dismayed to learn that none were stocked. Certainly, there were plenty of books, plenty of CDs, plenty of T-shirts, plenty of small plastic animals, but not one thing about native beadwork. I was told to travel down the road to another museum, which I promptly did. In their gift shop, I found not only beading books and supplies, but also a delightful woman from the local tribe who was willing to share some techniques and stories about her beadwork (which I also bought). Moral of the story: Why let visitors spend $100 or more at the "place down the road" because your gift shop doesn't match the experience?

—Lisa Brochu

PTs (pre-trash) as a way to make money, it may be best not to do it. In fact, it can detract from the experience or override your message.

At the Warm Springs Indian Museum in central Oregon they tell the stories of three tribes of the Paiute nations. Beadwork is an important part of the decorative trappings of these people and their gift shop sells a variety of materials for doing beading. The sales clerks sometimes do beading projects as they wait for customers, leading to conversations about beading. This is the kind of relationship that retail items should have to the organization. Books, craft kits, educational toys, bird feeders, and other items related to the central theme and sub-themes of your site can be very appealing to your customers. If you don't provide such opportunities, they will seek out private businesses and spend their money with them. Human nature dictates this need for memorabilia. Your philosophical objection to sales items in general will not affect how a guest behaves, so why not capitalize on the desire for memorabilia by ensuring that sales items help tell your story and generate revenue for your own site in the process?

Granted, finding high-quality retail items can be a challenge. The Association for Partners with Public Lands (APPL) has a trade show each year for natural and cultural history associations that includes 150 to 200 vendors for natural and cultural history stores. It is a great location to meet diverse vendors at one time

Case Study

In the late 1980s I was director of the Greenway and Nature Center in Pueblo, Colorado. We had decided to do a Dinosaurs Alive exhibit with Dinamation, Inc. that used robotic dinosaurs. We combined the exhibit with interpretive guides, naturalistic settings, and a gift store, using a building at the Colorado State Fairgrounds for our temporary dinosaur museum. We designed our floor plan with the museum store in one corner of the building by the exit, easily accessed. I made a trip to Amarillo, Texas, two weeks before we opened to see a Dinamation exhibit in action and I asked their staff what they had learned from the experience. They had designed the gift store as we had and then later moved it so that everyone exited through the store. Their sales volumes and profits increased ten-fold with that simple move. Most museums at that time had learned that it's unreasonable to expect each person who goes through the store to buy something, but an average income tends to be about $1.75 per person who actually enters the store. If the doorway to the store is to the side of the exit, perhaps one in ten people will go through it. If they exit through it, all will go through and your gross sales will be ten times as much. Dinamation provided a very high-quality variety of PMI type books, games, and toys to sell. They were educational and provocative. The store was really fun to visit alone and some in the community did that. We moved our museum store so that all exited to it and it became a very important part of the revenue stream for that very profitable event. Location is important thing in museum store planning but be sure you sell truly educational memorabilia as well. If you consider this crass commercialism and choose to not sell things, your customers will buy their plastic dinosaurs at the local discount store, which means that you've lost money that could have been spent on additional programming at your site.

—Tim Merriman

and learn the basics of retail merchandising. Location of sales areas, display techniques, and pricing are as important as product selection and talking with others who have experience can help you make the right choices.

Placement of a sales area makes a significant difference to the bottom line. Ideally, people visiting your site should see the sales area as they enter the facility and actually exit through the retail store. If you have chosen items that recall the experience or enhance the educational value for the customer, then you are simply extending that experience through the offerings in your sales area. In other words, your sales items are also interpretive media and can help promote or reinforce your message. Visitors who have enjoyed their stay will most likely want to see what you have to offer as memorabilia. Think about the retail shop as an extension of the visitor experience and make it match the theme and quality of all you do. Many of your customers will thank you for helping them find the right PMI to follow up the visit. And those who aren't interested can simply walk through the store and exit without a purchase.

Training your store staff to act as interpretive hosts will also contribute to the experience. If staff know some of the history behind the selection of certain items for sale and how they relate to the site theme, or can steer visitors to purchases that create connections with the visitors' interests in the resources, then time spent in the gift shop becomes part of the entire thematic experience.

Retail profits will usually vary from thirty percent to fifty percent on most items. Books are usually sold at double the purchase price. Profits can be plowed back into more programs or staff, allowing you to continue to enrich the experience for your guests. Don't forget that your audience is the same one who shops at REI, Barnes and Noble, Krispy Kreme, and other experience economy businesses. They tend to expect you to have things to sell. They want memorabilia.

Logo Items

Retailing offers another opportunity to show the organizational brand. When clothing items display your logo, sales items match the exhibits and programs, and ambiance fits well with the visitor experience, you are building the brand of your agency or site. Logo items become very appealing to those who have strong positive feelings about their experience. When these people wear your site's logo items, they become walking billboards for the organization. If the logo has been designed to reflect the site's central theme, suddenly the important message you want to share is being observed and interpreted to people who haven't even visited the site. When others ask about the apparel, the experience is repeated by the wearer. Word of mouth is always the most powerful form of advertising and logo clothing and items can encourage it.

Logos on apparel add value to the item in a variety of ways if the brand is thematic. People will tend to pay more for an attractive item that means something to them, as well as getting your site's message out to others. It should indicate something about the feeling of the experience and give an indication of the resource. If your logo is not that appealing, think about redesigning it to better match the vision for the organization. Design your graphic images with logo clothing and branded material in mind. Make images clean, clear, and workable in many forms. Simplified variations of of the logo might be designed for use on items that have limited space.

It is important to buy high-quality items to display your organization's logo. If it falls apart in a month, the message can be negated. Select quality items for your logo line of apparel or memorabilia.

Premiums

Premiums are gifts to customers that also can serve as PMIs. These can be given to members in a membership packet that might include such items as window

Good managers will require concessionaires and buyers to avoid stocking
junk that can be purchased at any dime store, as was found at this nationally
known site.

stickers, patches, pens, and cloisonné pins. They can be gifts given for donations,
including shirts, jackets, backpacks, tote bags, fanny packs, art prints, posters,
books, and calendars. They provide another chance to display the logo and show
the brand off to your most enthusiastic customers. Plan them with thought and
care. Members will treasure items given to them as awards, donor gifts, and
volunteer rewards. They will be displayed or worn for years by constituents,
enabling the recipients to talk about the experience they have had with your
organization. Make these items work for the organization by selecting things that
thoughtfully match the experience and the feeling of the organization. You will be
glad you did when a decade later you see premium items from your first campaign
proudly displayed by one of your loyal members.

The National Association for Interpretation gives awards and premiums to
members that are made from natural stone material by Stone Imagery, a
commercial member of the organization. These quality art pieces are more
appealing than the mass-produced plaques offered by most organizations and it
shows off the good work of a member, making them a winner in two ways.

Marshall McLuhan, a communications writer, said in his book *Understanding*

Media (1964), "The medium is the message." We communicate with everything we do. Develop your post-marketing icons, retail stores, logo items, and premiums with care. They are some of the positive cues related to the theme and sub-themes of your organization. You can make a lasting impression with these important media.

9

Professional Recognition

Professional Awards

Agency awards programs provide incentives for performance improvement by individual staff members employed by that agency. They become part of the corporate culture (see Chapter 10) by rewarding innovation and excellence on the job. Many agencies also participate in regional or national awards programs that involve nomination of outstanding employees from each area who are then reviewed by a panel of judges, leading to the selection and recognition of one exceptional individual in the agency each year. The National Park Service's Freeman Tilden Award, Army Corps of Engineers' Hiram H. Chittenden Award, USDA Forest Service's Gifford Pinchot Excellence in Interpretation and Conservation Award, Bureau of Land Management's Excellence in Interpretation and Environmental Education Award, and U.S. Fish and Wildlife Services's Sense of Wonder Award are presented each year at NAI's National Interpreters Workshop.

Many professional organizations also offer award programs for recognition of excellence by individuals or institutions that hold membership in the sponsoring organization. The National Association for Interpretation's award program consists of regional, section, and national awards in a variety of categories. These annual awards provide the opportunity for colleagues and supervisors to publicly recognize those people who serve their organizations well.

Certification

Recognition of individual interpretive professionals and interpretive sites by a national or international organization through a certification or accreditation process provides an opportunity to measure performance against standards set by an impartial peer review. Although these terms are often used interchangeably, for the purposes of this book, *certification* will be used to describe the process for recognition of an individual and *accreditation* will be

NAI's first recognized Certified Interpretive Guide class was held in La Paz, Mexico, in December 2000. Four years later, guide classes had been held throughout the United States and on four continents.

used to describe the process for recognition of a site or agency.

The certification program of the National Association for Interpretation is gaining acceptance worldwide as the standard for individual performance in the interpretive field. The organization struggled for decades to develop a meaningful certification program for its members. Surveys of the membership indicated that roughly one-third of the members strongly desired a certification program, one-third flatly refused to participate or support such a program, and the remaining third were unopposed to implementing a certification program as long as it remained voluntary. After much debate about how to create a meaningful program for the many varied individuals who make up the membership of NAI, the program finally became a reality in 1998.

Initially, the program consisted of four professional categories: Certified Interpretive Manager, Certified Interpretive Planner, Certified Interpretive Trainer, and Certified Heritage Interpreter. A job analysis of the NAI membership revealed that most professional members could reasonably attempt to meet the standards established for those categories. Eligibility requirements for these categories include a bachelor's degree in something

NAI trains trainers to deliver the Certified Interpretive Guide and Host programs to your staff and volunteers, using your own site's resource content to augment the interpretation and customer service techniques taught in the courses.

related to interpretation or four years of field experience (paid or volunteer). The certification requirements are designed to recognize existing skill levels and include an open-book exam, an essay exam, and submission of evidence of practical applications of job skills appropriate to each category. Materials submitted by the applicant are examined by a panel of three peer reviewers and must pass a rigorous evaluation before certification is granted. Participants in the program have commented that going through the process allowed them to assess where they were in their professional development and identify areas of weakness.

Each of these categories has an optional training workshop associated with it. Participants are able to complete several of the requirements for certification during the workshop. The workshops, scheduled by the National Association for Interpretation, also provide an opportunity to hone existing skills and perhaps learn new ones.

In 2000, a discussion with the Federal Interagency Council on Interpretation revealed that almost 500,000 volunteers, docents, seasonals, and new hires were on the front line providing interpretive services with little or no experience or

**Profiling the
Interpretive
Profession**

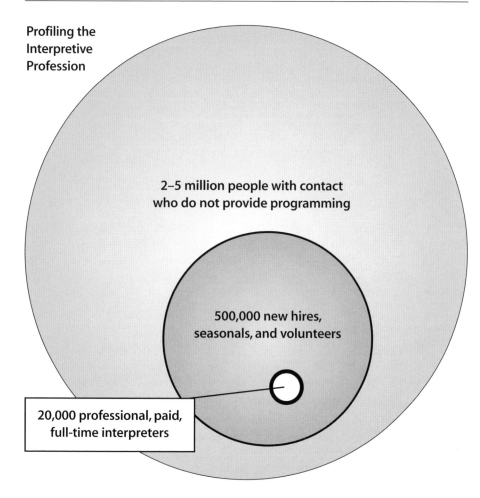

2–5 million people with contact
who do not provide programming

500,000 new hires,
seasonals, and volunteers

20,000 professional, paid,
full-time interpreters

training in techniques or philosophy of interpretation. This discovery led to the
creation of a fifth category and the development of a training program for
front-line interpreters who deliver programs. The Certified Interpretive Guide
category requires that applicants be at least sixteen years of age. Applicants
must complete a thirty-two-hour training workshop taught by a Certified
Interpretive Trainer sanctioned to use NAI's curriculum materials. During the
workshop, participants complete a presentation outline and deliver a ten-minute
thematic presentation based on the outline. They receive coaching on technique
and are exposed to some of the best literature in the field by taking an open-
book exam. Over 2,000 individuals became Certified Interpretive Guides within
the first thirty-six months of the program's beginning.

As more agencies began using NAI's CIG program as a standard of
performance for beginning interpreters, the need to address another aspect of
interpretive site operations became apparent. In 2002, Texas Parks and Wildlife
Department provided funding to assist NAI in the development of the Certified

Interpretive Host program. This sixteen-hour training workshop is designed to help those who have public contact at interpretive sites but who don't conduct formal presentations. Maintenance workers, receptionists, ticket takers, volunteers, law enforcement, security guards, and sales clerks benefit from the training that combines techniques of informal interpretation with customer service. The result is a staff that understands their role in helping the agency achieve its mission while turning every visitor contact into an interpretive opportunity.

Certification in all six categories offered by NAI lasts for four years. Recertification requires evidence of continuing education in the field to encourage constant professional development. Individuals can be simultaneously certified in any categories for which they are qualified. Other professional organizations offer certifications for specialties such as exhibit design (Industrial Design Society of America), landscape architecture (American Society of Landscape Architects), environmental education (North American Association of Environmental Educators), and a variety of other professions that might be of interest to those who work for or with interpretive sites.

Accreditation

Many interpretive sites can be accredited through a professional organization. Accreditation programs generally review a site's operations and programs, scoring them against a set of common standards. Zoos look to the American Zoo and Aquarium Association for accreditation standards while museums use the Museum Assessment Program designed by the American Association of Museums and camps subject themselves to the rigorous review standards set by the American Camping Association. Often, a particular type of site that wishes to be accredited must use the best available program if a specific evaluation program has not been established for that type of site. For example, nature centers wanting to evaluate their operations have looked to the Museum Assessment Program although that program was not specifically designed for nature centers.

Why Certify?

The benefits of certifying individuals or accrediting agencies or sites are many. Individuals find that certification helps them evaluate their own effectiveness and improve their performance. Because many agencies now require certification of interpretive professionals, individuals who have been certified find that they are more competitive in the marketplace when looking for employment or advancement. Those individuals who successfully complete the certification process testify to their sense of personal pride in accomplishing a benchmark in their professional development.

Agencies who have adopted certification or accreditation programs as standards within their operations soon learn the value of having staff at different levels and in different positions that all share a common vocabulary

NAI's Certified Interpretive Host training ensures that every volunteer and staff person contributes to the mission of the site through their communications with visitors. (Pictured: Tokyo National Museum)

and approach to interpretation. Going through a training process together is an exercise in team-building that continues to yield benefits long after the workshop is over. The trust and respect for colleagues that develops during an intense training or site review effort serves the agency well by creating corporate culture.

Creating Culture

Have you ever worked somewhere and felt like a stranger in a strange land? You simply did not feel comfortable or fit in. Organizations, like countries, develop cultures. Like an unknown country, the culture can feel friendly and welcoming or it can be a very exclusive club with a sign that says, "No Entry." As an organizational manager and leader, you can create the culture or you can simply sit back and see what happens. What are the chances of accidentally developing a culture that is welcoming and supportive of staff and members if you simply "let it grow?" You might get lucky, but the culture may be dysfunctional to some degree if you do not guide the process.

Treat your staff as you hope to have them treat members or customers. Is it unlikely that your staff will treat customers as honored guests if staff members are allowed to treat each other disrespectfully. You give the culture a definite head start if you take time to listen to your staff, know them, and show an interest in their advancement, growth, and well-being.

Example is not the main thing in influencing others, it is the only thing.
—Albert Schweitzer

Great managers take great pride in showing an interest in their employees as people, not just as workers. That attitude sends a clear message about how to treat customers. Like Freeman Tilden's interpretive principle about interpreting to the whole person, we need to understand employees as whole people who have home lives, dreams for the future, desires to advance, and their own ideas about how to run our organization. Listening is a valuable skill to practice and it begins by withholding judgment and just being open to the ideas of others.

Staff Retreats and Meetings
Listening to employees informally on a daily basis is critical but attempts to listen and share ideas formally are equally vital. Holding regular staff meetings,

at least monthly, perhaps weekly if possible, is a good practice. A small staff can meet as an entire group, while that may be more challenging for very large staff groups. It may be more feasible to meet at the departmental level if your staff numbers in the hundreds.

Meetings should have an agenda that permits input by any employee before the meeting or when it begins. Some organizations rotate the facilitation or chair role for staff meetings to give individual employees a sense of ownership. It is also important to set a finite time limit on staff meetings and conduct business on time. That also sends a message about your values as a manager. You value your employees' time and that of the organization. Business should be orderly and efficient.

Staff retreats away from the usual business location are perhaps the most useful. Within the office environment, the temptation to pull away from the meeting and attend to the telephone or other business can quickly take precedence over the point of the retreat. A staff retreat is a wonderful place to conduct long-range planning, address troublesome issues, and brainstorm new strategies for old problems. Don't limit it to business, though. Devise ice breakers, "get-acquainted" games, and team-building activities to reveal the personalities of employees and allow them to bond in ways unrelated to the organization. Taking a high adventure trip together or even going to the theater as a group can break down communication barriers between employees who cannot seem to connect at work.

Branding

Your organization can have a "brand" identity for your members, customers, or users. You have to determine what that will be through planning your central theme. Every aspect of the organization identifies the brand message and delivers the theme: the logo, the facilities and grounds, the uniforms, the signage, and especially the behavior of staff.

A conservation organization that lacks a recycling program creates a conflicting message. An aquarium that tells people that plastic bags are dangerous to sea turtles and then forces you to take a plastic bag in the gift store defeats its own message and makes its mission statement seem shallow. A historical facility with furniture of inappropriate time periods has created interference for its story.

Quality matters very much in branding. When someone mentions theme parks, you probably think of Walt Disney World first because they set a very high standard. If you want that kind of "brand" recognition, you must be very consistent in providing very high-quality services. There are several ways to insure that level of quality.

Uniforms

Placing staff in uniforms helps employees identify with the theme of the organization while giving comfort to the customer. The uniform style, color, and components matter very much. They should convey the theme, be comfortable for the kind of work being done, and present the desired image. Polo shirts and shorts look and feel right at a recreational facility. A wet suit or swim clothes might be the right uniform at a water park or marine park. A blazer and tie or historically themed costume can be just the right look at a presidential library or historic site.

It is most important that uniforms be clean and well kept, used consistently, and set the tone for the property. They create the first impression for the customer. If the first impression is not a good one, the entire organization is stuck with trying to overcome that negative image for the rest of the visit. It's a tried and true old saying, "You never get a second chance to make a first impression."

Appearance

Employees also make a statement about the organization by how they look, smell, and behave at first meeting with the customer. The uniform or lack thereof may make the first statement but hygiene, personal jewelry, body art, and demeanor fill in the blanks.

Hygiene may be one of the most challenging issues to discuss with employees. One way of hosting the discussion at a staff meeting is to play a very simple game. Take four empty metal cans or plastic zipper-type bags and fill each with cotton. Liberally soak the cotton in one with a cheap perfume, another with water-soaked cigarette butts, another with smelling salts and the fourth with a couple of drops of liquid soap. Pass each around and have staff members sniff the contents. Ask which is the preferred scent for our organization? Discuss the impact on customers of staff members who have the personal odor of strong tobacco, body odor, or cheap perfume. Your staff will likely find the gentle smell of soap more appealing and the exercise makes the point if followed by the discussion.

Jim Covel, director of education at Monterey Bay Aquarium, tells his volunteers that they should not be more interesting than the resource. When they are good interpreters, the experience is not about them, it is about the resource. If the interpreter has six earrings, blue hair, or two-inch-long fingernails, the attention of the guest is usually on the speaker instead of the resource. Most organizations concerned about professional image will set reasonable standards for appearance regarding personal jewelry, hair styles, and visible body art, applying the rules fairly and consistently. When interviewing, it is important to give prospective employees a clear understanding of the policies related to personal appearance and hygiene. It is also important to help them understand that although you respect their right to look and act as they wish on their own time, the standards of your workplace will be observed at work. If they are not prepared to comply, do not hire them.

Training

Have you ever started a new job only to be handed keys to an office and a stack of uniforms and asked to "go to work" with only the job description for the position

The information desk is your best chance to make a good first impression. Put yourself in the place of the visitor and test the appearance and attitude of your information desk and the people who staff it.

as your guidelines? This approach has become so common among natural and cultural resource organizations that most of us are amazed if something more elaborate happens. The Disney Corporation is well-known for its theme parks and incredible hospitality, but the magic doesn't just happen. They make it happen by training workers before putting them in front of the public. They are quick to point out that it only takes one rude employee to ruin the legendary "Disney experience." Workers must know what to expect and understand the mission and themes of your organization if they are going to deliver those to the public with clarity and in a friendly way.

Training has never been more essential than it is today in heritage interpretation. As interpreters we are entrusted with the Earth's most sacred stories, history of the planet, history of diverse peoples, and the discoveries of science and the arts. Sending novice interpreters, docents, and volunteers out to the meet the public and represent our agencies with no training makes it almost certain that they will deliver muddled messages. As a manager, you may think the message being conveyed is one of conservation, stewardship, and wise use. The public may be receiving a message that seems more like "have fun, spend

Encouraging creative problem-solving techniques can build a better team effort among staff. Here, a group tries to untangle a human knot.

money, and take what you want as long as no one's looking."

In 2001, the National Park Service (NPS) in the United States hired a public relations firm, Ogilvy Public Relations Worldwide, to analyze messages the public receives at national parks. Ogilvy's study compared those messages to the intended messages of the agency. There were many gaps between the messages the NPS wanted to deliver and what members of the public were receiving, so the NPS began a messaging project with a central theme of "Experience Your America." This and other messages and practices developed in the program are now used more consistently through the agency. However, more than one half million volunteers and docents now work in the U.S. on the front-line, conducting personal interpretation programs or providing informal interpretive services. About 44,000 represent the NPS at 388 sites. Without consistent training of all front-line workers, including volunteers, the messages you want delivered may never reach the customer.

It is valuable to have thematic messages on non-personal items such as exhibits, Web sites, and brochures, but employees are the most important communication resource in conveying themes. Helping people connect with the resource and understand the central theme of the interpretive facility will happen most easily if those conducting programs are trained in thematic personal interpretation. NAI offers a Certified Interpretive Trainer (CIT) course to help your agency's staff members become sanctioned to teach the Certified Interpretive Guide course to your employees or others. Some CITs train front-line workers from other organizations and use the fees they are paid to underwrite the costs of training their own staff members.

Front-line workers who do not lead hikes or do personal programs are also capable of turning a "ho-hum" experience into the trip of a lifetime for one of your guests. The maintenance worker who tells a family at a zoo the time when the animals will be fed and suggests the best viewing location may turn the visit into something very special. The cashier at a store who notices a customer buying books on a certain topic and suggests other books or resources will light up the face of a guest. Law enforcement personnel who help guests understand the reasons for rules can change their attitude more easily to being compliant. NAI's sixteen-hour Certified Interpretive Host Course provides this vital training for all workers who meet and greet the public at an interpretive facility. This course is also taught by CITs who have taken NAI's CIH Trainer course. It is designed to get all front-line employees to be skilled at hospitality services as well as informal interpretation. They can change a guest experience from one of frustration to one of transformation, thereby helping the organization accomplish its mission.

As a manager, you may enjoy teaching and want to be the trainer. However, if that's not your talent or interest, you may help those on your staff with those talents become the in-house trainer. You might also hire others to train for you. When budget cuts come, as they almost always do, training is the last place that you should cut corners. Think about that for a moment. If you are going to downsize and ask the same staff to do more with fewer resources, skill levels must be enhanced. If you cut staff off from training by not approving travel or access to training, you send the wrong message to them and leave them less well-equipped to handle their increased responsibilities.

Celebrating Success

What are your traditions as an organization for thanking employees and volunteers when objectives are met, milestones are reached, or things just go well for another year? If you don't have these built-in celebrations, start thinking about when and how to celebrate success.

Everything you do or forget to do in the organization establishes culture. If the organization ignores employee morale and tolerates whining as the usual behavior, you are not going to keep the most enthusiastic, turned-on employees. They will seek friendlier workplaces. Breaking from work for a birthday party, to recognize an individual's achievement, or to observe a milestone set in the long-range plan will tell everyone that he or she is individually important and their work matters. Most people who work in this field do not work just for a

Case Study

The difference that training your staff as interpretive hosts and guides can make in a guest's experience speaks volumes about whether you are achieving your goals as a manager. My sister recently visited Alaska for the first time. She described two experiences to me—a boat trip to see glaciers and a bus tour of Denali National Park. The boat trip she simply wrote off as the "kind of experience that makes you never want to take a packaged tour again. Ever." From the time the guests were ushered immediately to the bowels of the boat for a mediocre chicken dinner (instead of being allowed to absorb the magnificent views) to the drone of the uninformed guide who clearly was misstating facts, everything about the boat trip spoke of a poorly trained staff and ill-conceived experience. In contrast, the bus tour guides at Denali National Park have been trained in NAI's CIG and CIH programs. Her e-mail to the Aramark regional manager summed up the difference:

> I can't begin to tell you what a profound experience the park tour was for me. The mountain was out and so were the animals. Clay Walker's presentation of the park added a sense of the holy to our time there. His scientific knowledge, communication skills, gentle humor, and intimate connection to the region richly enhanced our sampling of the secrets of Denali. He is like his name, "the earth walker," and knowing him for a day impacted us. I'm sure you are aware of the value he brings to your team.
>
> I have read the interpretive book you gave us several times. It is a great tool for reinforcing our experience. As a visitor, I found myself unwilling to spend any time in museums/visitor centers when such spectacular real life was just outside. Even meaningful outdoor signs would just litter the view. So on this first trip, my interactions with Alaska were more sensory than intellectual. But in Denali, a guide like Clay and a book like the one you provided helped bring the whole package together.
>
> Thank you for undertaking the professional mission of sharing Denali with visitors like me while preserving it for its inhabitants and for future guests.
>
> —Amy Simpson

Enough said. Training matters.

—Lisa Brochu

Providing extra touches that meet basic needs such as the loaner umbrellas at the Tokyo National Museum help guests have a more memorable visit.

paycheck. Your employees likely want to make a real difference in the protection of natural and cultural resources and in connecting the public with natural and cultural heritage.

How do you celebrate success? Do something that matters to your staff. If they enjoy pizza, throw a pizza party. If they like cookouts, hold a luncheon barbecue in the outdoors. Find out what works with your culture and staff and build some funds into the budget for celebrating success. Help your staff understand that you value them and want to reward their best efforts, even in little ways. It's not about how much you spend. It's about taking time to say thanks and to celebrate!

Performance Rewards

One very important way to reinforce the best behaviors with staff is to say thanks in a more formal and useful way. This can be a day or days off for meeting objectives for the year or a cash bonus if your system allows that. When a bonus is given based on spending less than was budgeted or bringing in more income than expected, it encourages those desirable behaviors. Each person on staff has a reason to save the organization money. You can allot a percentage of any surplus at year end to a bonus pool and find an equitable way to distribute it among all staff. Be sure you reward those who do support roles for staff as well as those who meet the guests.

If rules restrict the payment of bonus cash or extra days off, find other creative ways, such as gift items donated by friends of your organization or excursions as a staff to do something fun together like rafting, skiing, movies or theater. Extending these rewards to volunteers and docents at an annual dinner or picnic is also valuable. You can use the awards to reinforce the positive quality traits you want your employees to have.

We talk about Maslow's Hierarchy of Needs in interpretive training because it is essential in the communication business to understand the motivation of people. It is also important to understand what drives your staff. They must be well-compensated, thanked for their good work, and recognized when performing exceptional work if you want to keep them on your team for a long time.

Branding the organization and creating a friendly culture is not an accident. You control what happens as the manager. Talk to your staff about quality, train them to be the best, and reward them in appropriate ways. Much like the golden rule, treat them as you hope to be treated by your administrator.

Membership Development

To have members, or not have members—it is a question whose answer matters a great deal. Other important questions to ponder when considering membership include:

Do we need advocates for our organization, people to support us politically?

Do we need a donor base that will give money predictably?

Do we have a specific group of audiences identified who want our programs?

If the answer to these questions is no, then a membership may not be necessary. However, few interpretive organizations will answer no. Constituent support is critical for not-for-profit organizations and has also become important to tax-supported organizations, as they seek gifts to cooperating associations or charge cost-recovery program fees. Governmental and not-for-profit organizations need political support as well. Memberships can be a key link to significant audiences for your organization. Memberships offer several advantages, including:

Identifying user and support markets clearly. User markets are those families or individuals who attend your programs, buy your products, and enjoy your facilities. Individual, family, and senior memberships are the more common categories used. Support markets are groups of people who are likely to support your programs without always expecting to get direct benefits. Often they join to show their support or subsidize your services for their customers or constituents. Commercial and institutional categories are commonly used to distinguish groups with different interests. Schools or other not-for-profits might join with institutional memberships while commercial memberships might be businesses who appreciate your mission or feel their constituents also use your services.

Maintaining communication with constituents in a clear, useful way. A monthly newsletter, Web site, and an annual report keep members informed about your programs, challenges, and successes. Print items create tangible benefits for people. It is vital to use photos and specific names in the publications to thank constituents in ways that can be seen by their friends and family. Publications must be delivered on time and at a high level of quality if they are to be effective. Relying on only one communication method may create problems if some individuals do not have access to that method. For example, assuming that everyone can easily gain access to the Internet and your Web site may not be looked on favorably if most of your membership is made up of senior citizens who prefer print materials. Occasionally conduct a random check of members to ensure that they are getting and using your communications. You may need to revise your methods or do damage control with constituents if they are not.

Allowing feedback easily from important audiences. A membership is a continual source of useful feedback that allows you to fine-tune programs. You should ask them how you are doing at every opportunity and thank them in as many ways as is feasible for their support. Focus groups and member surveys provide useful information about programs and facilities.

Giving members a sense of ownership. Members donate money and, as donors, expect and must receive recognition. Donor plaques, donor lists in the annual report, and monthly donor recognition in a newsletter are all ways to recognize gifts. Members-only special events are another way of making members feel like insiders. Volunteer programs are powerful because they allow members to function in staff roles and represent your organization without the long-term responsibilities of taking a job. This sense of ownership is valuable but you must be clear about what donors and volunteers must do and what they get for their contributions. Sometimes they have unrealistic expectations about what they should be able to influence or what benefits they should receive. Provide training and written policies that make their roles and rewards clear. Volunteers become a very important political constituency in times of crisis, for they often know the organization as well as staff, but have the freedom to react as citizens.

Making donor solicitations easy. Members expect to be asked for money and time. You must find respectful ways to do that, but need not be timid about asking. Some organizations ask their memberships to donate as many as thirteen times a year while most ask for renewals of memberships once a year and seek donations to an annual gifts campaign one other time a year. After only a couple of years, you develop a sense of how much income constituents will provide, allowing donations to become a regular part of the annual budget. Levels of giving may ebb and flow somewhat due to the economy but they are actually more predictable in most cases than program income.

Membership Structure

There are several ways to create a membership structure. You may be able to determine the most appropriate membership model for your site by answering these questions:

Publicly recognizing donors in creative and thoughtful ways can promote further donations by others. The Texas State Aquarium uses native limestone to create a stunning backdrop for its donor panel.

What categories will best separate market segments according to similar program interests? Membership organizations often make up membership categories without thinking about how the categories might function. Lumping seniors and students might make sense in terms of the amounts of the fee, but they generally do not share program interests so you probably will want separate categories for them. Corporate members are very different from institutional members because the former will often be willing to cosponsor events and donate funds to support individual groups such as students, while institutions usually want a more favorable fee structure, recognizing that they are often not-for-profits or government entities, functioning more like a partner than a donor or sponsor.

What services/benefits will we provide with perceived value of the costs for membership? The perceived value of a benefits package should seem to be worth more than what is paid for membership. When a family pays $40 a year for a family membership, it often expects discounts for programs, free passes to events, and similar member benefits that will exceed the cost of the membership. The family usually uses those free services less than they expect but the perception of net gain is important to them. Seniors will often insist on a discounted membership and then make very generous donations in the annual campaign. They feel they have earned the right to discounts as elders of the tribe, and yet they are often more likely to have a philanthropic spirit about giving, especially if you time your requests well.

How will we recruit members? Every contact with your natural audiences is a chance to recruit members. Member discounts help people to decide to join when attending a specific event. Giving people a two- or three-month membership when they pay to attend a program is a way of getting them into the database to see your publications. Dr. Bob Thomas, former executive director of the Louisiana Nature and Science Center, had a membership blank printed on the back of his business cards so that he could hand out a mini-recruitment form with every card.

Usually membership income alone does not yield net income to support programs or facilities. You have to reinvest most of the income in member benefits. The net effect is positive despite this seeming pass-through of money. You can ask members for support as donors several times a year in several ways and those funds support the organization's new initiatives and long-term development. But making the benefits substantial is essential if you expect to hold the members you recruit. Their advocacy may be vital to the organization surviving during difficult times.

Membership Services

Membership services vary widely but some basic services should be considered for any constituent-based organization. They are:

- Free or discounted access to fee-entry grounds or events

- Discounts for fee-based programs

- Member publications—newsletter, annual report, program flyers

- Discounts in gift or bookshops

- Members-only events—annual dinner, volunteer recognition activities, etc.

- Member premiums—bumper stickers, logos, patches, key chains, etc.

- Member trips—ecotours to distant places or even field trips locally with an expert

- Specialized member services unique to the organization—early bird sales at an arboretum's annual plant sale, early bird preview of a new film at a museum

A membership manager or specialist should be one of the first two or three hires for a professional staff of a membership-based organization. This person usually manages the database for the membership and coordinates diverse member services. As an organization grows, this function becomes a key department with multiple staff because serving constituent needs well is vital to maintaining this core revenue source.

Specialized donor services usually will be developed as an organization becomes large enough to have development specialists on staff to conduct planned giving or bequest programs. Members will often be willing to name a beloved not-for-profit organization or public organization with a "friends" group in their will if approached properly and assisted with the technical requirements. Boiler-plate language for bequests in wills is available on a wide variety of Web sites and may easily be found using search engines with key words "bequest" and "language."

Communication Strategies

Members must hear from you regularly and in a variety of ways to feel engaged and a part of the "family" of the organization. Some of the specific communication devices and their roles follow:

Newsletter and Web Site

- Inspirational stories about the resources and members

- Recognition articles to praise donors or simply list their names (use bold type for names to make them stand out in text)

- Program calendar

- Donor appeals, wish lists, volunteer opportunities

- Contact information

- Registration forms or procedures for classes, programs

- Photos of donors, volunteers, program participants

- Policy changes, seasonal hour changes, explanations of rules

- Online registration or orders (Web sites only)—shopping cart or interactive forms

Phone Calls

- Reminder calls to program registrants

- Follow-up calls to new members to make certain they are getting services

- Personal invitations to "Members Only" events

- Customer satisfaction survey—brief interview to get feedback

Annual Meetings and Reports

An annual meeting is often a requirement of membership organizations if stated in the bylaws. Though this meeting may fulfill some state requirements of not-for-profit corporations, it is also a great idea from a communications standpoint. The annual meeting provides a chance for all members to get together and hear an inspirational presentation on the status of their investment. The president and executive director usually use this opportunity to thank key donors and recognize volunteers with awards. It may include a program by a guest speaker of national or regional stature. It might also include fun or recreational events, such as a dance, costume ball, black tie affair, art show, or trade exposition.

An annual report may or may not be required by bylaws but is always a good idea. It becomes another formal location to thank members and donors. It should be done so attractively that it also functions as a stand-alone report on the organization to foundations and government partners or oversight groups. Annual reports usually include:

- President's report

- Executive director's report

- Treasurer's report—audited balance sheet and income/expense statement

- Photos from key events and programs

- Donor lists

- Graphic depictions of services, statistics, and milestones

- Grants report

Annual Giving and Capital Campaigns

The two most common fund-raising activities conducted with memberships are annual giving campaigns and capital campaigns. They tend to be less effective if combined. Because they have different specific roles, they may be more effective if spaced well apart.

Annual Giving

This campaign is designed to offer members a chance to donate above and beyond regular membership. Many or even most of your members may not participate each year. A persuasive letter from the president, executive director, or both of more than one page is advisable. Single page pleas have been found to be less effective than more detailed letters of two pages. The letter should talk about the vision of the organization and include some specific achievements of the organization leading to the vision. Though statistics are useful in talking about levels of achievement, it is important to make a passionate appeal. The commitment of members to the vision of the organization is often more emotional than intellectual. They often will respond best to specific stories about people they know or local situations they understand and care about. For example:

Case Study

At the Greenway and Nature Center of Pueblo in Colorado, we used volunteer trail rangers, mostly senior citizens, to patrol the city bike trails and provide assistance to users. They were asked to patrol in four-hour time blocks. During one hour of that period we asked them to rest and conduct two different kinds of simple user surveys. The first was observational. They simply noted what people were doing—walking a dog, fishing, jogging, etc., by making tick marks on a checklist. Their count of the varied uses and quantity of people provided valuable data about customer preferences. They also were trained to conduct simple five-question customer interviews with the public to find out what they liked, did not like and how often they used the trails and related services. The survey activities gave volunteers a desirable break in the middle of a block of patrol time and the data collected was useful to our understanding of visitor uses and preferences. This method of collection of data was virtually free and analysis could be done by staff or local college students as part of a class. The data was vital in planning and decision making through the years.

—Tim Merriman

You are helping protect the homes and food for many kinds of local wildlife by supporting the Friends of Forest Lake.

You might make very specific pleas if you can translate gift amounts into levels of commitment to organizational goals. For instance:

Your gift of $500 supports an injured bird of prey for one full year.

Or

Your contribution of $500 will guarantee that 100 additional children from the community will have access to museum programs this coming year.

Member contributions to annual giving and capital campaigns are essential. Corporate and foundation gift givers will look at your record of gifts from members to judge how important your organization is to your constituents. If your members and board of directors are not substantially committed to your fund-raising drives, organizations who do not know you well do not feel compelled to give. Many groups compete for funds. Foundations and corporate donors use amounts and numbers of member gifts and board gifts to evaluate your effectiveness locally.

Capital Campaigns

Capital drives are specifically oriented toward building funds, capital equipment acquisition, or endowment development. These appeal to some people more because they seem more long-lasting. It is important to develop donor materials with language that projects the vision of the organization. "We are building a solid foundation for the future of our organization" is more appealing than "we are building a brick and steel structure that will last for a long time." As in good interpretation, you can use themes in capital fund-raising that connect people from the tangible benefits of a building or exhibit to the intangible universal values of "strong foundation" or "our long-term dreams of a home for conservation of … ."

When soliciting "capital," you are usually raising restricted funds. You are telling the donor that the money will be used specifically on a building project or as part of an endowment. Your statements to that effect label the money as "restricted funds" from the point of view of accountants and the Internal Revenue Service. They are tracked separately in your bookkeeping and reported as "Restricted Funds" in your audit reports. You most show a clear paper trail for use of the funds using GAAP Standards (Generally Accepted Accounting Practices). It is best to have an external audit each year by a Certified Public Accountant or accounting firm that reports on your management practices and affirms your account balances in both restricted and unrestricted areas.

Government organizations will have their own mandated procedures for this, but not-for-profits must create the financial policies and guidelines that assure members, donors and foundations that you handle their funds responsibly.

Building Campaigns

So-called "brick and mortar" campaigns to finance a new building, new wing, or specific exhibit will attract people who want substantial tangible benefits for their contributions. Images of a new building based on architectural elevations, physical models, and virtual tours on a Web site can make a building or exhibit project come alive for donors.

Donor names on a plaque, founder's clubs, and other methods of recognizing major donors create lasting value. Imaginative techniques employed for recognition include murals with people's names, bricks with engraved names, walls with donor names and, of course, dedication of the entire project or exhibit to a specific key donor. You can name an amount of a gift that will allow a donor to be recognized forever with naming the project for their family or themselves. Donor plaques can be designed within the organizational theme, such as a wood-carved mural with the names of donors carved into the border or even picture. The Warm Springs Indian Museum in Oregon has a beaded donor recognition hanging that is quite attractive and depicts their skills as bead artists.

Endowments

An endowment is a restricted investments fund created to yield interest, dividend, or growth revenue to support programs and projects. When you solicit these funds for an endowment, you should have a board-approved endowment policy in place that assures donors and auditors that you will never touch the investments for operating expenses. This "corpus" or body of the endowment is legally protected as a restricted fund. Your organization may have a standing financial committee or executive committee that oversees financial management but it is usually wise to have a separate investments committee to manage the endowment fund. Those who give will expect this committee to be a decision-making body that makes conservative choices to protect their funds in perpetuity and yield profits to the organization. Real estate, mutual funds, equities, bonds and Treasury bills are some of the many investment instruments used to produce income from an endowment.

Each endowment campaign should have an annual objective with a very specific amount of money to raise. The target should be a stretch amount that will not be easy to make but is attainable. A volunteer committee who will raise the funds should have a staff liaison person, usually the executive director, development director or development specialist. A general rule of thumb suggests that you will raise ninety percent of your funds from ten percent of your donors so large gifts from a few key people are essential to a successful campaign. Most often it works best to have committed donors ask new donors who are peers to give. If you have a donor who has given $100,000 to a campaign, he or she will be more successful in making this size request from another donor with whom she or he is well-acquainted.

Many organizations believe that establishing an endowment fund will keep their organization financially healthy far into the future, but the reality is that few organizations have large enough endowments to rely solely on the endowment income for operating expenses for any length of time. While establishing an endowment is almost always a good idea, diversifying income streams is an absolute necessity for maintenance and growth of any organization.

Methods of Solicitation

Both annual and capital campaigns can be approached in similar ways. Typical methods of soliciting funds are:

- Direct mail

- Donor Web sites

- Donor-get-a-donor

- Sponsorships (attached to specific project components)

Memberships are a method of turning key audiences or target markets into "insiders" who know your vision for success and want to help achieve it. You have a responsibility to communicate with them and give them value for their contributions. If you fulfill your commitments, they will be long-time supporters and will help insure the long-term success of your organization.

Databases and Tracking

A good database is essential for keeping track of member names, addresses, and categories. Ideally you want something powerful enough to allow you to also track donations and giving habits. Though any database software, such as Access or Filemaker Pro, on a PC or Macintosh will work, these programs require extraordinary user knowledge to be made compatible with a bookkeeping system. Some commercial software designed for not-for-profits integrates bookkeeping with a donor database (i.e. Quickbooks Enhanced for Not-for-profits—PC users only). These work best because they make external audits easier. This kind of software also expands as your membership grows, and that is important. Bookkeeping software packages often have a finite number of client records, which can become a problem at some point in the growth of your organization.

Keeping comments about each donor can also be valuable. Knowledge of their family affiliations, interests, past giving record, and recognition preferences can save you time and trouble in preparing for donor events. Merge mailings allow you to customize the information in thank-you and recognition letters to state the specific amount given. This information is required annually by the Internal Revenue Service and is best done just after start of the new year to give donors a record of total gifts for the previous tax year.

Be sure that your database tracks total gifts over time and not just within a specific campaign. Donors usually remember well how much they have given and want to be recognized in a donor category that shows cumulative gifts. Several software packages exist that make donor tracking easy and some integrate with bookkeeping systems. DonorPerfect and iMIS are two of the better known packages available for PC computers.

Government Friends Groups

Government-owned nature centers, zoos, aquariums, museums, and historic sites often create or encourage development of a "friends" group or natural/cultural history cooperating association as a partner to accept donations. The mission of the not-for-profit defines its role in support of organizational programs. Usually the bylaws and articles of incorporation can be developed from boilerplate documents from similar organizations. However, it is important to review boilerplate bylaws to be certain they reflect the kind of relationship the not-for-profit will have with the government agency. When audited by the Internal Revenue Service, the bylaws and mission set the guidelines for evaluating expenditure of funds.

Not-for-profit partners can take donations, develop membership structure, and train volunteers to assist the governmental operations. Often they not only develop revenue from memberships but handle specific other functions that governmental employees may not be allowed to do such as gift store sales.

Profits or surplus from "friends" groups are restricted with some organizations to specific support activities, such as interpretive services, for the governmental entity. They may be unrestricted and managed by the not-for-profit board in cooperation with a liaison person from the governmental agency. If you are the government liaison person, you must invest time in oversight if you want the "friends" group to truly be your friends. They will have good ideas and want to help so meeting with them regularly to get their feedback is important.

An annual workshop hosted by the Association for Partners in Public Lands is a valuable network for those working with or managing friends groups.

Conclusion

Few of us go into the interpretation field with a wild desire to be a manager. It's more likely that we want to save the planet, inspire our audiences, and enjoy the delight in a child's eyes when a new discovery is made. Somewhere along the path we learn that managers are better paid, allowed to make critical decisions, and really can influence the amount of good, inspirational work that gets done.

You are reading the last section in the book, so you have persevered through the material or you're that special maverick who starts at the end so you know where you will end up. Either way it is important to remember that the end of the book is just the beginning of another book or seminar or management course. The world is full of good resources for learning management skills, but most of them are not focused on the interpretive field. We encourage you to delve into the material that has been created for corporate America and apply what you learn to your own site when appropriate. It may mean looking at resources beyond the bookshelves you normally visit, but you'll be glad you did. When you quit growing as a manager, you lose the chance to discover new ways of improving the programs, products, and services that connect people to the resources of your site.

Most managers find some enjoyment in management. When the demons of budget shortfalls, political games, and crises are in retreat, it can feel very good to be in charge. When we exceed our own expectations with measurable objectives, it is especially exciting. It's fun to set "stretch" goals and objectives and land beyond them. It's especially wonderful when the results are paid in the currency of our earlier work—the bright eyes of children, the return of rare wildlife, and the preservation of historical treasures.

Good managers empower their employees, volunteers, and audience members to grow and discover more on their own. As interpretive managers, you remove barriers that allow them to see, feel, and experience their world and the stories owned by their culture. You can open up the path to wonder by being great at what you do. You manage an interpretive site and can be proud when you do it well. What you do matters.

Each new morning brings a new opportunity. As a professional in this field, you bring a personal responsibility to work each today. You not only must do your best but share your best. You learn the most when you teach others. Take your management skills to professional meetings, in-service trainings, and networking opportunities to share what you have learned. Challenge yourself to make a difference, and you will.

Index